INTERNATIONAL STUDENT MINISTRY

I-DIG

INTERNATIONAL DISCIPLES GROUP

AN INTRODUCTORY SMALL GROUP DISCIPLESHIP GUIDE
FOR INTERNATIONAL STUDENTS & SCHOLARS

by
KRISTA MARTIN, ERIC WU,
& KATIE RAWSON, EDITOR

Published by InterVarsity International Student Ministry

© 2013, 2015 InterVarsity Christian Fellowship/USA

ISBN 978-0-9835848-3-4

Graphic design and cover artwork by Laura Li, twentyonehundred productions

Scripture quotations marked (NIV®) are taken from the HOLY BIBLE, NEW INTERNATIONAL VERSION ® NIV ® Copyright © 1973, 1978, 1984, 2011 by Biblica, Inc.™. Used by permission. All rights reserved worldwide.

Scripture quotations marked (CEV) are from the Contemporary English Version Copyright © 1991, 1992, 1995 by American Bible Society. Used by Permission.

"The Big Picture" is taken from Passport to the Bible by Fred Wagner. Copyright © 1999 by InterVarsity Christian Fellowship/USA. Used by permission of InterVarsity Press, P.O. Box 1400 Downers Grove, IL 60515. www.ivpress.com. "The Big Picture" was written by Katie Rawson and includes material shared by Paul Hoffman, Stanley Klassen and Bill Syrios.

"Cultural Tips for Communication" is taken from I-GIG: A Guide for International Groups Investigating God. Copyright © 2005 by InterVarsity Christian Fellowship. This I-GIG tool is copyright © 2004 by Janet Payne and used by permission of Janet Payne.

The exercises for practicing the presence of God in chapter four come from Joe Moore, InterVarsity Co-Director of Spiritual Formation and Prayer.

The "Broken" diagrams are a revision of an earlier version entitled "Broken Family" by Katie Rawson. Many thanks to Rev. Al LaCour, Eva Liu Glick, Matthew Graff, Annelies Van Brocklin, Eric Manela, Beth Lindahl, and Krista Martin for valuable feedback during the revision process.

A special thanks to ISM Department Director and ISM Daniel Project Director Lisa Espineli Chinn for initiating this project and for crucial feedback during the editing of the field-test edition.

Many thanks to Nate Mirza of the Navigators; Mayumi Pohl of Second Level, a discipleship ministry for Japanese; and Al LaCour of Reformed University Fellowship International for reading the field-test edition and providing helpful suggestions for revision.

Thanks to Eva Liu Glick, Matthew Graff, Bonnie Ward, Johnny Mettlach, Pastor Ricky Poon, Jovin Adjeitey, and Tammy Gonzaga for feedback on initial chapters.

Thanks also to the InterVarsity ISM staff who shared feedback and field-testing results: Matthew Graff, Beth Lindahl, Karla Meyers, and Brian Hart.

A special thanks to Pastor Douglas Griffin, who wrote some of the "Word and Concept List" entries and gave valuable feedback on all of them.

And many thanks to InterVarsity Writer/Editor Lisa Reich who proofread the final version and suggested helpful changes.

CONTENTS

CHAPTERS

TOOLS

CONTENTS

DISCIPLESHIP & DIGGING: INTRODUCTION TO THE *I-DIG* GUIDE

My grandmother[1] used to sing an old song with a verse in it that has remained in my mind since childhood:

> I'd rather have Jesus than silver or gold;
> I'd rather be His than have riches untold;
> I'd rather have Jesus than houses or lands;
> I'd rather be led by His nail-pierced hand.[2]

As a widow trying to make a living on a small farm, she didn't have much silver or gold, but her love for Jesus influenced me deeply. She treasured the Bible, and I still remember family prayers with her at bedtime. It was the way she lived her faith in everyday life, though, that impacted me the most. She continually shared food and clothing with needy neighbors.

In the days before she died I heard her calling the name of Jesus, and I think she saw him while still on this earth, as Stephen (one of the early Christians) and many others after him did.

My grandmother was a **disciple**[3], an everyday follower of Jesus. Relationship with Jesus and life in his family were her treasures, not silver or gold. In fact, the old song that she loved so much uses a word picture that can teach us a lot about discipleship: treasure. In Matthew 13 Jesus tells the story of a man who finds buried treasure:

> The kingdom of heaven is like treasure hidden in a field. When a man found it, he hid it again, and then in his joy went and sold all he had and bought that field. (v. 44 NIV)

What kind of treasure would make someone so joyous and excited that they would sell everything they have for it? Jesus says that living in God's family and under God's rule (the **kingdom of heaven** or **kingdom of God**) is worth giving up everything you have.

---

[1] This article was written by Katie Rawson.
[2] The song is "I'd Rather Have Jesus" and the lyrics are by Rhea F. Miller.
[3] Words in **bold color** in the text are in the "Word and Concept List" on p.127.

7

Your *I-DIG* guide is a manual for international students and scholars seeking the treasures of following Jesus (discipleship) in the cross-cultural family of God. "I-DIG" is short for International Disciples Group. An I-DIG is a group of internationals from one or more cultures who want to grow together as disciples of Jesus. We recommend a group size of three to five people. Keeping the group all female or all male will allow trust to grow more quickly and will facilitate deeper sharing, so consider that option as you put your group together.

Jesus' first disciples grew by watching and listening to him in a group. Jesus is not with your group in person, but you can meet Jesus together as you discuss and obey God's Word! The *I-DIG* emphasizes studying and memorizing parts of the Bible because these are tested ways of meeting Jesus. The following habits will help you take in and grow from the Word:

COMMUNITY: God's plan is for you to become disciples in community where you can benefit from the modeling and encouragement of others. Discussing the Bible in a group will help you understand and obey it better.

PRACTICE: Spiritual practices or disciplines, such as time alone with God and memorizing Bible verses, help you "make space" in your lives for God to change you. These practices help you live out what you discussed from the Word and become the kind of people who follow God by habit.

ACCOUNTABILITY: Checking up on each other and praying for one another as you obey the Word and try out these practices will help you stay on track in the discipleship journey.

We use the inductive method of Bible study in the *I-DIG* so that you can learn to discover what a Bible text means without the help of a teacher. **Inductive Bible study** enables you to draw your own conclusions from a text. It has three parts: observation, interpretation, and application. Since we have chosen Bible passages from many parts of Scripture, we suggest that each group member read through "The Big Picture" (p.15) to get a sense of the entire story of Scripture.

PEOPLE TREASURES & CULTURAL TREASURES

As if the treasure of the kingdom were not enough, there is another field of treasure to explore as well as you meet together: the people in your group and the cultures that have influenced you all! Revelation 21 pictures heaven as a city, the New Jerusalem:

> Nations will walk by the light of that city, and kings will bring their riches there. The glorious treasures of nations will be brought into the city. (vv. 24, 26 CEV).

I believe that the treasures of the nations are facets of various cultures that reflect unique aspects of the image of God. Just as each person is created in the image of God, cultures—which are created by people—also reflect the image of God.

The image of God in people and cultures has been spoiled by sin, of course. So digging for treasure in cultures requires careful thinking about how our cultures are and are not in line with what God teaches. A cross-cultural group is a great place to do that kind of thinking, because we can often see the blind spots in our own cultures better when we are exposed to other cultures. As we develop trust and friendship, we may be able to gently point out some of the blind spots we see in the cultures of our friends.

So the *I-DIG* will often ask your group to consider how the *thinking, values, and behavior in the culture you are currently living in and in the culture you grew up in either agree with or oppose what you learned from the Bible* that week. This skill—critiquing cultures in the light of the Bible—will help you and your group distinguish true treasure from false and begin to see how your cultural background has influenced you both positively and negatively.

People from different cultures communicate differently, of course. If your group contains folks from a variety of cultures, "Tool A: Cultural Tips for Communication" (p.13) will help you connect with each other well. It takes all groups a while to build trust. Keep answering the questions as honestly as you can, and trust between you will grow.

My grandmother gave our family a great treasure by her example of following Jesus every day in good times and bad. It was a much greater treasure than money or jewels. Our world desperately needs to see communities living life the way Jesus would. The authors of the *I-DIG* are praying that God will use it to help you uncover treasures in God and in each other. And we pray that you, in turn, will point other people to the treasures of being a disciple and start communities of disciples who live like Jesus.

GETTING THE MOST OUT OF YOUR *I-DIG* GUIDE

Welcome to your I-DIG group! Committing to help one another grow during a specific time period can be very powerful for group members. To help you get the most out of your group experience, we encourage each new I-DIG group to read and agree to the following practices. Some groups actually sign this page to show their commitment.

We will:

- ◑ participate in a one-and-a-half-hour meeting once weekly for twelve weeks. (Some groups may decide on one hour per week with a little more homework).

- ◑ listen well to other members of the group.

- ◑ share our thoughts freely but not dominate the discussion.

- ◑ stay focused on the Bible passage or topic being discussed.

- ◑ keep everything group members share inside the group.

- ◑ memorize the memory verse and practice the suggested discipline each week.

- ◑ pray for one another in-between group meetings.

- ◑ encourage one another and challenge each other to put into practice what we are learning.

- ◑ celebrate our group experience at the end of the twelve weeks.

- ◑ prayerfully consider finding two or three others whom we can lead through the same material once we have completed the *I-DIG*.

- ◑ decide on a group time, place, and dates.

God is really the one who makes disciples, so prayer for one another is crucial. The following prayers from the early Christian missionary Paul are a wonderful model for us. Try putting them in your own words and praying them often for yourself and your fellow group members:

▶ **EPHESIANS 1:17–19 (NIV)** I keep asking that the God of our Lord Jesus Christ, the glorious Father, may give you the Spirit of wisdom and revelation, so that you may know him better. I pray that the eyes of your heart may be enlightened in order that you may know the hope to which he has called you, the riches of his glorious inheritance in his holy people, and his incomparably great power for us who believe.

▶ **EPHESIANS 3:17B–19 (NIV)** And I pray that you, being rooted and established in love, may have power, together with all the Lord's holy people, to grasp how wide and long and high and deep is the love of Christ, and to know this love that surpasses knowledge—that you may be filled to the measure of all the fullness of God.

THE I-DIG GROUP MEETING: A PREVIEW

 OPEN gives group members a chance to share how obedience to the previous week's passage, the practice of the spiritual discipline, and memorization of the verse went. Spend 15 minutes on this part (10 if your meeting is only one hour).

 DIG IN is the Bible discussion time. Take 55 minutes (35 for a one-hour meeting) to read the introduction and go through the questions. The week's facilitator should decide in advance which questions are essential and which can be omitted if time runs short.

 RESPOND contains instructions for a practice that will help you apply the study to your life and as well as a memory verse chosen to help you remember the topic of the study for the week. Spend 20 minutes (15 for a one-hour meeting) reading the instructions for the week's discipline, going over the memory verse, and praying together.

 DIG DEEPER includes suggested studies to help you go deeper into the subject or "customize" the topic for people from different cultural backgrounds. You can do these studies during the twelve weeks or return to them later. Some of them will fit into your daily time alone with God. For those who lead a new group of friends through the I-DIG after finishing the material yourself, "Dig Deeper" will help you go more in depth on the topic so that you can be even more prepared to lead others.

The "Guidelines and Notes for Facilitators" section found in the back of the guide has important notes for the first meeting and for each additional one. If you are the facilitator, read it before the first meeting and each week as you prepare the chapters.

If you have only one hour to meet, here are a few tips:

- ◗ Keep your group size small, three at the most.

- ◗ Have everyone read the chapter introduction under "Dig In" and then read and mark the Scripture text as suggested in question two in each study in advance. You can each do this during one or two of your times alone with God each week.

- ◗ Focus on the questions with an asterisk* as you go through the Bible discussion.

CULTURAL TIPS FOR COMMUNICATION

We all want to communicate clearly. This is especially true if we are speaking with people whose home language and culture are different from our own. We may feel that we are missing the right words or that our pronunciation is getting in the way. We repeat ourselves and check for understanding. However, even when we are comfortable with our language, we can still have communication problems. Listen to what these people are thinking:

> ANN: How boring! She just sits there and doesn't say anything.
> *MARY: How rude! She talks and talks and never lets me say a word.*

> JOE: He's not listening. He won't even look at me.
> *JOHN: The way he looks at me makes me uncomfortable.*

What can we do with problems like these? The best answer is to go out of our way to show interest and respect as we speak. However, we have different *ways* of showing interest and respect. Our style or pattern of communication can differ from culture to culture, family to family, and yes, even between men and women. These differences often cause us to send – and receive – wrong messages. But if we see the problem, we can make small changes to adjust to the other person's style.

ADJUST YOUR STYLE

VOLUME Try speaking a little louder or softer.

BODY LANGUAGE Try looking at the person when he is speaking to you, or stop looking so directly at him if he seems uncomfortable.

S P A C E Try standing a little closer or further away.

PACE Pace has to do with timing. Here we mean the time we wait between one speaker and the next. Some people speak as soon as someone else finishes and others wait several seconds. The first group thinks "jumping in" shows you are interested, and the second group thinks the others are rude. If you are in the first group, try W..A..I..T..I..N..G for others to speak. (Count to ten.) If you are talking with those who jump in, learn how to jump in politely. Watch what happens when you do!

JUMPING IN

Um... Let me see... Just a sec... Excuse me. I have something to add here... Um, I have a question about that... Could I interrupt for a second? Could I go back to something you said?

SHARING & DISAGREEING

In my opinion... It seems to me... My feeling is... What if...? Actually... Well, actually... Another way of looking at this is... I am not sure I completely agree.

CHECKING

Do you (Did you) mean...? ...Can you give me an example of that? ... I'm not clear on that, could you explain it to me? ...Let me see. You said... Could you say more about...?

ENCOURAGING

Do you have the same opinion? ...Do you agree? ...What's your point of view... You haven't had a chance to talk. What do you think? That's a great idea... I like that idea because...

 COLOSSIANS 4:6 (NIV) Let your conversation be always full of grace, seasoned with salt, so that you may know how to answer everyone.

"Cultural Tips for Communication" is taken from *I-GIG: A Guide for International Groups Investigating God*. Copyright 2005 by InterVarsity Christian Fellowship. This *I-GIG* tool is copyright © 2004 by Janet Payne and used by permission of Janet Payne.

THE BIG PICTURE

The word *Bible* comes from the Greek word *biblia*, which means "books." The Bible contains sixty-six books, written by at least forty different authors over a period of at least 1,500 years. The oldest book was written about 1400 B.C. or earlier. The last book was written about A.D. 100. When we read the Bible in English, we are reading a translation of material originally written in Hebrew (the Old Testament or first part of the Bible) or Greek (the New Testament or second part of the Bible). The events described in the Bible take place in the lands north and west of the Persian/Arabian Gulf and surrounding the Mediterranean Sea.

Although the biblical books are written in different styles and reflect different cultural backgrounds, the authors believed that what they wrote was uniquely inspired by God; their words are God's message to all people.

THE TWO TESTAMENTS

There are sixty-six books on the "The Bible at a Glance" chart. The first thirty-nine books, from Genesis through Malachi, are grouped in a section called the Old Testament. The last twenty-seven books, from Matthew through Revelation, are called the New Testament. Testament is another word for a will or **covenant**, a legally binding promise. The Old Testament describes God's covenants with the Jewish people and his promise to bless all nations of the earth through them. The New Testament shows how this promise was fulfilled in Jesus Christ.

Despite covering over 2,000 years of human history, the Bible has a theme that unifies all of its sixty-six books. The Bible tells us what God has been doing in human history and the purposes for which he created us. The Bible's story can be viewed as a drama in five scenes.

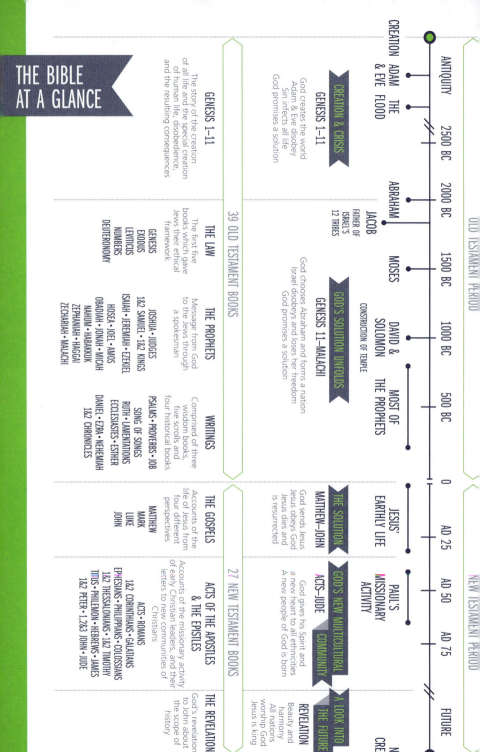

THE BIBLE AT A GLANCE

Timeline: ANTIQUITY · 2500 BC · 2000 BC · 1500 BC · 1000 BC · 500 BC · 0 · AD 25 · AD 50 · AD 75 · FUTURE

CREATION · ADAM & EVE · THE FLOOD · ABRAHAM · JACOB (FATHER OF ISRAEL'S 12 TRIBES) · MOSES · DAVID & SOLOMON (CONSTRUCTION OF TEMPLE) · MOST OF THE PROPHETS · JESUS' EARTHLY LIFE · PAUL'S MISSIONARY ACTIVITY · NEW CREATION

CREATION & CRISIS
GENESIS 1–11

God creates the world
Adam & Eve disobey
Sin infects all life
God promises a solution

GENESIS 1–11

The story of the creation of all life and the special creation of human life, disobedience, and the resulting consequences

GOD'S SOLUTION UNFOLDS
GENESIS 11–MALACHI

God chooses Abraham and forms a nation
Israel disobeys and loses her freedom
God promises a solution

GENESIS 11–MALACHI

39 OLD TESTAMENT BOOKS

THE LAW
The first five books which gave Jews their ethical framework

GENESIS
EXODUS
LEVITICUS
NUMBERS
DEUTERONOMY

THE PROPHETS
Message from God to the Jews through a spokesman

JOSHUA • JUDGES
1&2 SAMUEL • 1&2 KINGS
ISAIAH • JEREMIAH • EZEKIEL
HOSEA • JOEL • AMOS
OBADIAH • JONAH • MICAH
NAHUM • HABAKKUK
ZEPHANIAH • HAGGAI
ZECHARIAH • MALACHI

WRITINGS
Comprised of three wisdom books, five scrolls and four historical books

PSALMS • PROVERBS • JOB
SONG OF SONGS
RUTH • LAMENTATIONS
ECCLESIASTES • ESTHER
DANIEL • EZRA • NEHEMIAH
1&2 CHRONICLES

THE SOLUTION
MATTHEW–JOHN

God sends Jesus
Jesus obeys God
Jesus dies and is resurrected

GOD'S NEW MULTICULTURAL COMMUNITY
ACTS–JUDE

God gives his Spirit and a new heart to all ethnicities
A new people of God is born

A LOOK INTO THE FUTURE
REVELATION

Beauty and harmony
All nations worship God
Jesus is king

27 NEW TESTAMENT BOOKS

THE GOSPELS
Accounts of the life of Jesus from four different perspectives

MATTHEW
MARK
LUKE
JOHN

ACTS OF THE APOSTLES & THE EPISTLES
Accounts of the missionary activity of early Christian leaders, and their letters to new communities of Christians

ACTS • ROMANS
1&2 CORINTHIANS • GALATIANS
EPHESIANS • PHILIPPIANS • COLOSSIANS
1&2 THESSALONIANS • 1&2 TIMOTHY
TITUS • PHILEMON • HEBREWS • JAMES
1&2 PETER • 1,2&3 JOHN • JUDE

THE REVELATION
God's revelation to John about the scope of history

NEW MISSIONARY ACTIVITY

SCENE 1 — CREATION & CRISIS, GENESIS 1–11

The Bible opens with the statement, "In the beginning God created the heavens and the earth" (NIV). The point of the Bible's teaching is not to prove that God exists, but to teach us what God is like. The story of our creation is one of beauty and harmony. Everything God made was good. The first human couple, Adam and Eve, were created for relationship with God, to obey him and enjoy him as his children. The harmony God intended is seen in the picture of a garden beautifully described in Genesis 2.

The picture was ruined when Adam and Eve chose to disobey God. Their life of harmony was shattered—not only with God but inside their hearts, with each other and with the earth. The Bible calls this refusal to trust and obey God **sin**. In choosing to disobey God, Adam and Eve chose to turn from God and live apart from him, acting according to their own wishes. Not only did this dishonor God but it separated them from the source of all life, and so they experienced spiritual death—and eventually physical death as well. Ever since, all humans have acted just as their original parents did, and so death, spiritual and physical, has become part of all human experience.

God's earth was afflicted by this deadly virus called sin. But God's love for his creation did not change; he promised a cure for **sin**. A child would eventually be born to a descendent of Eve. This child would take the punishment for sin on himself (see Genesis 3:15). The rest of the stories in this first part of the Bible show how God protected the earth from total pollution by sin.

SCENE 2 — GOD'S SOLUTION UNFOLDS, GENESIS 12–MALACHI

This section contains the beginning stage of God's plan to repair the damage done by human disobedience. Around 2000 B.C., God chose one human, Abram (later renamed Abraham), and promised that through his son and grandson God would form a nation: Israel. The Jews, Abraham's descendants through his son Isaac and grandson Jacob, would be God's special people to keep alive knowledge about him on the earth. The stories of how God cared for Israel point ahead toward God's solution for the human problem. God dramatically rescued Israel from slavery in Egypt around 1500 B.C. This rescue was a picture of what he intended to do for all humans through Jesus, the Messiah, or deliverer, whom he would send. God also communicated his laws to their leader Moses so that they would know how to live healthy and harmonious lives.

Despite all God did, Israel's history reflects the human problem of distrust and rebellion toward God. When God first gave them their own land, they frequently turned from God's laws and did what was right in their own eyes. They were not content to live under God's rule. They asked for a human king in order to be like other nations. When their kings listened to God and followed his ways, they had peace and well-being, especially during the reigns of David and Solomon, around 1000–930 B.C.

God placed Israel among various world powers so that they could be a lighthouse to all earth's people. God's intention was that Israel would model the peace and wholeness that come when people obey God's words. When Israel's great King Solomon built a temple where people could worship God, he knew foreigners would pray to God there. The great queen of Sheba visited Solomon and praised his God (1 Kings 10:9).

But Solomon himself, who was supposed to be the wisest man in the world, began to worship other gods at the end of his life. As a result, after he died his kingdom was divided into two nations, Israel and Judah. Both nations were conquered and taken into captivity—Israel in 722 B.C. and Judah in 586 B.C.

God did not give up on the people; he sent special messengers (prophets) to teach them how to live and remind them that the Messiah would come. To one of these prophets, Isaiah, who lived around 700 B.C., God gave amazing pictures of this Messiah.

SCENE 3 〈 THE SOLUTION, MATTHEW–JOHN

The New Testament continues the story of God's plan for his world four hundred years after the last book in the Old Testament. The first four books, or Gospels, announce the arrival of the Messiah. Each Gospel is named after its writer and describes the life, teachings, death and resurrection of Jesus Christ. Christ is the Greek word meaning "Messiah," the one first announced to Eve in Genesis and then to the **Jewish people** through the prophets.

Jesus taught that people could be born into God's family by believing in him. He also said that God's children should live in an attitude of love, serving others and forgiving even their enemies.

Jesus called twelve special men, the **disciples** or **apostles**, to be with him and tell others about him. But most of the religious leaders, including the leading priests and teachers of the Jewish law, did not listen to Jesus; they worked together to have him killed.

God's solution to the human problem of sin now became clear. Jesus, who never sinned, willingly died on a cross for the sins of all people who will look to him in faith. The punishment for sin is death, but God allowed Jesus to die for us as a substitute. Then Jesus was raised to life on the third day as a sign that he really is God's Son. Death was conquered and the power of sin was broken.

Jesus offers to give a new heart and a new spirit to anyone who will accept his gift of life. God forgives our sins, gives us his Holy Spirit to live inside us and promises us that we will be raised to new life with him after we die, not because of our own goodness but because of the goodness of Jesus. People may now once again live in harmony with God. (Jesus' death and **resurrection** occurred around A.D. 30.)

Beginning with Acts we read the story of God's new kingdom people. They are equipped to carry on the work of Jesus. They tell all peoples that the King has come and that he invites them to join his new community. The books that follow are letters from leaders of the early Christian church.

The most famous of these leaders is Paul. Although he was a Jew, he obeyed Jesus' command to tell the good news to people who were not Jews. Paul saw himself as an ambassador of God, and he wanted people to be reconciled to God through Jesus (see 2 Corinthians 5:20). Paul was beaten, shipwrecked and eventually killed because of his faith in Jesus. But at the end of his life he was able to say, "I have kept the faith. Now there is in store for me the crown of righteousness" (2 Timothy 4:7–8 NIV). Paul wrote these words before he was killed in A.D. 67 or 68.

SCENE 5 〈 A LOOK INTO THE FUTURE, REVELATION

The prophets or messengers of God in the Old Testament looked forward with hope to the return of the Messiah as King over everything. They thought it would all happen at one time when Jesus first came. Jesus taught that there are two comings. The first was God's coming to earth in the mission of Jesus to defeat sin and death. His second coming as King is still future. At that time God will remove all people who will not accept his Son as King. Everything will then be restored to the beauty and harmony pictured in the Genesis garden. People of every nation, tribe and language will worship God together (Revelation 7:9–10). The book of Revelation describes the events surrounding the return and crowning of Jesus as King.

THE RELIABILITY & AUTHORITY OF THE BIBLE

CAN WE TRUST THE BIBLE?

The reliability of the New Testament is what people question most. Document reliability is established based on the number of manuscripts we have and the dates of those manuscripts; the more there are, and the older they are, the more reliable the document is. For the New Testament we have

- 5,300 Greek manuscripts, 10,000 Latin manuscripts, and 9,300 other early versions

- 24,000 manuscript copies of the New Testament in existence today

- 230 manuscripts that were compiled before the seventh century

- letters written by the early church fathers, from which we can reconstruct the entire New Testament (minus 11 verses that are not crucial)

- archaeological evidence:

    Nelson Glueck, a Jewish Reformed scholar and archaeologist, was quoted as saying, "To date no archaeological discovery has ever controverted [contradicted] a single, properly, understood biblical statement."

    William F. Albright, a renowned archaeologist, says, "Discovery after discovery has established the accuracy of innumerable details and has brought increased recognition to the value of the Bible as a source of history[1]."

---

[1] These figures and quotes come from "The Bible: Document, Historical and Archeological Evidence of Its Absolute Reliability" by Jay Smith, quoted from the website study: "The Bible and the Qur'an: An Historical Comparison": *http://debate.org.uk/topics/history/bib-qur/bibmanu.htm* quoted at *www.biblestudymanuals.net/bible.htm*. Material about the Old Testament can be found in this article as well.

WHY DO WE GIVE THE BIBLE AUTHORITY IN OUR LIVES?

Christians believe that the Bible is the "word of God." This does not mean that we believe it was written by God's own hand. In fact, it's very clear that human authors wrote the various books, as the Bible is filled with each author's literary style, perspective, personality, and vocabulary.

But, even though humans physically wrote the Bible, the source of all Scripture is God, as the Bible itself indicates: "All scripture is God-breathed" (2 Timothy 3:16 NIV); "Your word is truth" (John 17:17 NIV); Jesus also affirmed the authority of Scripture by using it throughout his ministry:

- He quotes Old Testament Scripture when tempted by Satan (Matthew 4:1–11; Luke 4:1–13).

- He quotes the prophet Isaiah at the beginning of his ministry (Luke 4:14–20).

- He speaks about the importance of the Old Testament in one of his best-known sermons, the Sermon on the Mount: "Do not think that I have come to abolish the Law or the Prophets; I have not come to abolish them but to fulfill them. For truly I tell you, until heaven and earth disappear, not the smallest letter, not the least stroke of a pen; will by any means disappear from the Law until everything is accomplished" (Matthew 5:17–18 NIV).

Since Jesus gave Scripture authority in his life and words, his followers should do so also[2].

---

[2] Most of these points are taken from material compiled by J. L. West. For in depth information consult the InterVarsity Press books *Is the New Testament Reliable?* By Paul Barnett and *The Old Testament Documents: Are They Reliable and Relevant?* by Walter C. Kaiser.

CHAPTER
1

GOD *the* FATHER

OPEN

- Introduce yourselves.
- Discuss key points from "Discipleship and Digging."
- Read aloud and discuss the guidelines listed in "Getting the Most Out of Your *I-DIG* Guide" (p.10) and look at the time-use suggestions in "The I-DIG Group Meeting: A Preview" (p.11). As a group, agree to these guidelines and decide on your weekly meeting time and place.
- Pray for your time of Bible discussion, which we call "Dig In."

 DIG IN

The Bible is the story of God's pursuing love. It tells us that God created human beings for relationship with him. He wants our obedience, but more than that, he wants our love. Ever since the first people disobeyed God, human beings naturally run from him. We do not like to depend on him, obey him, or stay in relationship with him. We think we know what is best for our own lives. Again and again we find ourselves in trouble, like the two sons in the story you are about to read. But God keeps looking for us.

The story begins with a son asking his father for his inheritance while his father is still alive. He is so eager and impatient for the life he desires to live that he is not willing to wait for his father's death to receive his share of the family wealth.

*1. In your culture, what are relationships with fathers like? How would parents react to a request like the one this son makes?

*2. Take a few minutes to read through the texts silently. Mark words you do not know, items that impress you and questions you have. Also look for repeated words and ideas as well as contrasts.

This story is told to tax collectors, who were some of the most despised people in Jewish society during the time of Jesus. They collected taxes required by the Romans (who ruled over the Jews) and often became rich by collecting extra money. Jesus spent time with such people, along with others who were simply labeled "sinners." When the religious leaders of the time saw Jesus eating with such people, they questioned him and grumbled. Jesus told three stories to explain why he was eating with "sinners." Verses 3–10 include stories about a lost sheep and a lost coin.

LUKE 15:1–2, 11–32 (CEV)

¹ Tax collectors and sinners were all crowding around to listen to Jesus.
² So the Pharisees and the teachers of the Law of Moses started
grumbling, "This man is friendly with sinners. He even eats with them."

¹¹ Jesus also told them another story: Once a man had two sons. ¹² The
younger son said to his father, "Give me my share of the property." So
the father divided his property between his two sons. ¹³ Not long after
that, the younger son packed up everything he owned and left for a
foreign country, where he wasted all his money in wild living. ¹⁴ He had
spent everything, when a bad famine spread through that whole land.
Soon he had nothing to eat. ¹⁵ He went to work for a man in that country,
and the man sent him out to take care of his pigs. ¹⁶ He would have been
glad to eat what the pigs were eating, but no one gave him a thing.

¹⁷ Finally, he came to his senses and said, "My father's workers have plenty
to eat, and here I am, starving to death! ¹⁸ I will go to my father and say
to him, 'Father, I have sinned against God in heaven and against you.
¹⁹ I am no longer good enough to be called your son. Treat me like one
of your workers.'"

²⁰ The younger son got up and started back to his father. But when he was
still a long way off, his father saw him and felt sorry for him. He ran to his
son and hugged and kissed him.

²¹ The son said, "Father, I have sinned against God in heaven and against
you. I am no longer good enough to be called your son." ²² But his father
said to the servants, "Hurry and bring the best clothes and put them on
him. Give him a ring for his finger and sandals for his feet. ²³ Get the
best calf and prepare it, so we can eat and celebrate. ²⁴ This son of mine
was dead, but has now come back to life. He was lost and has now been
found." And they began to celebrate.

²⁵ The older son had been out in the field. But when he came near the house, he heard the music and dancing. ²⁶ So he called one of the servants over and asked, "What's going on here?"

²⁷ The servant answered, "Your brother has come home safe and sound, and your father ordered us to kill the best calf." ²⁸ The older brother got so angry that he would not even go into the house.

His father came out and begged him to go in. ²⁹ But he said to his father, "For years I have worked for you like a slave and have always obeyed you. But you have never even given me a little goat, so that I could give a dinner for my friends. ³⁰ This other son of yours wasted your money on prostitutes. And now that he has come home, you ordered the best calf to be killed for a feast." ³¹ His father replied, "My son, you are always with me, and everything I have is yours. ³² But we should be glad and celebrate! Your brother was dead, but he is now alive. He was lost and has now been found."

▶ **OBSERVE**

3. Discuss any words that are unfamiliar. Let one person retell the story with his/her own words.

4. What impresses you in the story?

▶ INTERPRET

Feeding pigs was a very shameful job for a Jewish person; the son cannot be in a worse situation. He plans to go home and ask to be a hired servant. Perhaps he thinks he can pay his father back for the wasted money! The father sees his son while he is still far off, meaning he is out looking. The father shames himself by leaving the house and running out to greet his son. He interrupts the son's speech and welcomes him. The robe, ring, and sandals are signs of sonship and honor. The older son insults his father and the guests by refusing to come in to the banquet, an action that was shameful. But the father humbles himself once again by leaving his guests and the banquet to talk with his older son.

*5. The younger son was expecting to become a hired servant and instead was treated like a son. If you had been the younger son, how would you have felt when your father treated you this way?

*6. What was going on in the mind of the older brother? What did he not understand about his father?

*7. This story, which would have been shocking to Jesus' hearers, is a very clear picture of **grace**, the unconditional and undeserved love of God. What was the lesson for the sinners and tax collectors?

For the Pharisees and teachers of the law?

▶ APPLY

*8. How does this picture of God differ from the ideas of God (or gods) in your culture?

From the idea of God you used to have?

9. When and how did you first come home to God?

*10. At different times, we can identify with the younger son, older son, or even the father. Which one do you identify with most right now?

Are there cultural, family, or personal obstacles keeping you from experiencing the Father's love?

What is the Father saying to you through this story?

*11. How does this picture of God the Father change your view of the **Christian** life?

RESPOND

Your practice for the week and throughout the 12 weeks of the I-DIG group is *daily time alone with God*. If you are not used to daily time with God, you can find some tips following this chapter. Each *I-DIG* chapter gives suggestions for Scriptures you can read during your daily time with God in **bold** print in the "Respond" or "Dig Deeper" section.

Adoration is reverent praise—our human response to God's amazing love for us. In your times alone with God this week, practice adoration by praying aloud **Psalm 103** and **other psalms** and using them to lead you into prayer. You can make them even more worshipful by changing pronouns that refer to God as "he" to "you." Other psalms that you can pray include **Psalms 145, 96, 98,** and **146.**

Read the memory verse together:

> 1 JOHN 3:1 (NIV) See what great love the Father has lavished on us, that we should be called children of God! And that is what we are!

Write this verse in your heart language here:

Memorize it in your heart language and in English this week.

- Memorizing helps you take in the verse at a deep level. God can use it to change you as you think about it over a period of time.

- Memorizing can help you obey God and defeat the enemy more easily.

- It can help you recognize lies being told in the world around you.

- Memorized verses help you remember God's presence and depend more on him.

HOW TO MEMORIZE SCRIPTURE

- Study the verse or verses and apply them in your life; ask God to write the Scripture on your heart as you memorize it.

- Get an index card and write the reference on the front and the verse on the back. Place the card in a visible place where you will be reminded to review it.

- Repeat the verse aloud often. Speaking aloud will actually help you memorize more accurately and remember longer.

- Review your verses daily and prayerfully think about them as you review.

DIG DEEPER

- If your relationship with your earthly father is distant or difficult, it may be hard to relate to the love and grace of God the Father. If this is the case, share this with an older Christian who can pray for and with you. And think about verses that talk about God's love.

- Matthew 6:9–13, the "Lord's Prayer," is the prayer of a well-loved child. Think about the various requests of this prayer and put them into your own words as you pray.

- Chapters one and two of *Losing Face & Finding Grace* by Tom Lin (InterVarsity Press) explore the implications of Luke 15:11–32 for people like the younger and older brothers.

- Timothy Keller's *The Prodigal God: Recovering the Heart of the Christian Faith* (Riverhead Books/Penguin) is a powerful look at the Father's love.

- *I Dared to Call Him Father: The Miraculous Story of a Muslim Woman's Encounter with God* by Bilquis Sheikh (Chosen Books) tells one woman's story of understanding God's Father-love for her.

SUGGESTIONS FOR YOUR TIME ALONE WITH GOD

TOOL
D

- Decide on a quiet place and time where you can be alone and focus on God, and then have your time with God at the same time each day. Many Christians find that starting their day with God is a great help in living as a disciple.

- Fifteen minutes per day is a good amount of time to begin with, but you may want to increase that time as you grow in the Lord.

- We recommend that you read Scripture and pray in your heart language precisely because it is your *heart* language. Communicating with God in your native language will enable you to grow closer to him and also better prepare you for living as a disciple back home.

- Spend 10–20 minutes reading through Scripture and listening for what God may be saying to you through the verses you read. Write down your thoughts about Scripture in a notebook.

WHAT TO LOOK FOR IN SCRIPTURE:

- **SIN** to confess
- **PROMISE** to claim
- **EXAMPLE** to follow
- **COMMAND** to obey
- **KNOWLEDGE** about God, self, or the world

- Spend 5–10 minutes praising God, confessing sin, thanking him, and praying for yourself and others. You can remember this order by thinking of **ACTS**.

- Write down your thanks and prayer requests and then go back and mark them when prayers are answered. If you are alone, pray aloud. This practice will keep your mind from wandering! If you're not alone, consider writing your prayers as letters or songs of praise, drawing pictures, or developing dance movements to worship God.

- For worship music in other languages, see the International Student Ministry section of the InterVarsity Store (*tiny.cc/ism-store*).

ACTS

ADORATION
CONFESSION
THANKSGIVING
SUPPLICATION
(humbly making requests)

CHAPTER 2

GOD *the* SON

OPEN

- How did you put into practice what you learned from the Word last week?
- How did your practice of adoration and time alone with God go last week?
- Take turns repeating the memory verse without looking at the guide.
- Pray briefly about what you just shared and for your time in the Word.

 DIG IN

Across cultures and throughout history, Jesus' character, life, and teachings have often been debated. In this chapter, we will explore Jesus' power and authority through a letter Paul wrote to the Colossians around 60 A.D. The Colossians were a group of **Christians** in Colossae, which is in present-day Turkey.

*1. Your picture of Jesus may have developed as your spiritual understanding has progressed. What words have you used to describe Jesus over the years?

How do you describe him today?

2. Take a few minutes to read through the text. Mark words you do not know and questions you have.

Paul is writing from a Roman prison to encourage the Colossians to remain true to what they know about Jesus Christ. There are some new teachings in Colossae that are false. The false teachers are saying that Jesus' power and authority are not enough to offer complete salvation. They believed that, to be saved, people should follow Jesus but also continue searching for secret truth and wisdom from other sources. Although the church in Colossae has witnessed some great fruit from sharing the gospel, they are tempted to believe these new teachings that deny the full authority and power of Jesus.

COLOSSIANS 1:15–23 (CEV)

[15] Christ is exactly like God, who cannot be seen. He is the first-born Son[1], superior to all creation. [16] Everything was created by him, everything in heaven and on earth, everything seen and unseen, including all forces and powers, and all rulers and authorities[2]. All things were created by God's Son, and everything was made for him. [17] God's Son was before all else, and by him everything is held together. [18] He is the head of his body, which is the church. He is the very beginning, the first to be raised from death so that he would be above all others. [19] God himself was pleased to live fully in his Son. [20] And God was pleased for him to make peace by sacrificing his blood on the cross, so that all beings in heaven and on earth would be brought back to God. [21] You used to be far from God. Your thoughts made you his enemies, and you did evil things. [22] But his Son became a human and died. So God made peace with you, and now he lets you stand in his presence as people who are holy and faultless and innocent. [23] But you must stay deeply rooted and firm in your faith. You must not give up the hope you received when you heard the good news. It was preached to everyone on earth[3], and I myself have become a servant of this message.

---

[1] The term "Son of God" is understood by some groups to mean that there was sexual intercourse between God and Mary. This is not true. The Bible teaches us that the Holy Spirit enabled a miraculous virgin birth when Jesus was born (see Luke 1:34–35).

[2] The unseen forces, powers, rulers, and authorities are angels. The false teaching in Colossae emphasized different levels of angels.

[3] Paul is using *hyperbole* (exaggeration to make a point) to emphasize how fast the gospel has been spreading.

▶ OBSERVE

3. Discuss any words that are unfamiliar. Retell the passage using your own words. What is the main point?

*4. What all do we learn about Jesus from this text?

▶ INTERPRET

5. What questions do you have? Answer the questions from the text and the context.

*6. What would this text have meant to the original readers—the members of the church of Colossae?

   How would they have been encouraged or challenged by this text?

▶ APPLY

*7. How does this text change your understanding of Jesus?

   What words will you use to describe Jesus now?

*8. How do verses 21–23 make you feel?

   When are you tempted to "give up the hope you received when you heard the good news" (v. 23)?

*9. What in this passage especially impresses your mind and heart?

   How do you need to respond to that this week?

RESPOND

This week, find a mature believer from your home country and talk about the ways you may be tempted when you return home to "give up the hope you received when you heard the good news." *Whom will you ask? How does she or he encourage you? What ideas does he or she give you to keep the hope?*

If you can't find someone from your country, look for someone from your region of the world or ask your staff worker to help you locate someone elsewhere in North America with whom you can talk on the phone or computer. If there are churches that worship in your heart language nearby, consider meeting with the pastor or another church leader.

Sometimes Christians need someone to encourage them and remind them of the truths of life with Christ, just like Paul did in his letter to the Colossians. In the future, when will you need this most? Read and memorize Colossians 1:17–18 as a way to help you remember the authority and power of Jesus.

 COLOSSIANS 1:17–18 (CEV) God's Son was before all else, and by him everything is held together. He is the head of his body, which is the church. He is the very beginning, the first to be raised from death, so that he would be above all others.

Write these verses in your heart language here:

Memorize them in your heart language and English this week.

Knowing how to share our beliefs about Jesus Christ is important for Christians! After this chapter you will find a set of diagrams called "Broken." This is a tool you can use to share your faith by highlighting the ways our relationships with God and each other have been broken.

Each day this week, work your way through the instructions for frames one through six of the diagrams by **reading the Scriptures listed below and thinking about them.** Knowing these diagrams will be useful to you as you meet people who want to know more about what you believe as a Christian. Make sure you understand each point and write down any questions you have about the diagrams in the margins to talk about next week.

FRAME 2: GENESIS 1–2   FRAME 4: PHILIPPIANS 2:5–8; JOHN 3:16

FRAME 3: GENESIS 3   FRAME 5: 1 CORINTHIANS 15:1–9, 20–23

FRAME 6: JOHN 1:10–13, 35–51

DIG DEEPER

- Learn more about **Jesus' deity and uniqueness** by reading the entry for it in the "Word and Concept List" on p.130.

- Knowing Scripture is so important for Jesus-followers! Studying and meditating on the Bible is a helpful way to root yourself in truth. The books of Matthew, Mark, Luke, and John contain the stories of Jesus' life here on earth. Choose one and read through it. Pay attention to Jesus' power and authority, as well as to his relationship to the Father and to the Spirit.

- There are groups today that also promote false teachings about Jesus. How do you distinguish a cult from a true Christian group? *They're Not Christian?* by Bill Perry answers this question. (It's available from Multi-Language Media, *www.multilanguage.com*.)

- *Is Jesus the Only Way to God?* by James Emery White (InterVarsity Press booklet) presents an important question that you need to have settled in your mind. Read John 14:6 and this booklet together.

- See *Jesus Among Other Gods* by Ravi Zacharias (W Publishing Group/Thomas Nelson).

- Muslim background believers can find help with the issue of Jesus being God in human form from an article located at: www.theabrahamconnection.org/Articles/DFY_Incarnation.html

INSTRUCTIONS FOR DRAWING & USING THE "BROKEN" DIAGRAMS

TOOL
E

These diagrams present God's good news (the gospel) in a way that makes sense to relationship-oriented people. They emphasize the honor and shame aspects of the gospel in order to give a more complete view than the Western outlines that focus on guilt or law. They also provide a way for you to share the gospel with interested friends—either people who are just learning about Jesus or those who seem ready to become followers. The most important points are printed in bold. We also suggest some questions you might ask your friends in order to make this more of a dialogue.

In the instructions below the large numbers on the left indicate what to say as you share these diagrams, and the numbered pencils in the diagrams show what to draw and in what order.

FRAME 1 BROKEN

1 **When we look around the world we see broken relationships everywhere:** between nations, people groups, families, and friends.

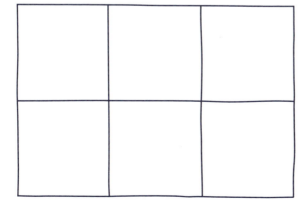

5 Where have you seen examples of broken relationships in the world?

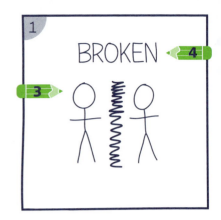

1 What do you think a world without broken relationships would be like?

We deeply desire that world without broken relationships; we yearn for harmony. The fact that we can imagine this world and yearn for it is a clue that we were made for it. In fact the Bible teaches that **God, the eternal Creator, who is Father, Son, and Holy Spirit, made human beings for relationships of harmony with him and each other.**

5 Human beings received life directly from God; relationship or harmony with God gave them life.

7 God honored them by giving them a special face-to-face relationship with him. The Bible tells us that the first man and woman were naked and yet not ashamed. Although they wore no physical clothes, they were clothed with the honor of God. They honored God with their hearts and they honored him by living in perfect obedience to him. So they both received and gave honor to God and to each other.

1 But the harmony the woman and man enjoyed was broken. When they disobeyed and dishonored God, relationship with him was broken, and soon the relationship between the two of them was broken as well.

4 When the relationship with God was lost, the man and woman also lost the honor they had received from God; they realized they were naked and therefore hid from God, feeling both shame and guilt.

6 Ever since then, human beings continually dishonor and break relationship with God and with each other. The Bible's word for this is sin. **Sin is the heart attitude that puts self first and dishonors and breaks relationship with God and people.** From this heart attitude come the individual thoughts and acts that are "sins."

8 Through sin, the man and woman also lost life; they were sent away from God's presence and learned that they would eventually die.

FRAME 4   **JESUS**

1 Human beings were in a state of separation from God. There was no way they could restore the relationship with God on their own because they could never honor or obey God perfectly no matter how hard they tried. Only God could make the relationship right again.

3 In families in some parts of the world, the older brother is responsible for the younger brothers and sisters and must seek them if they are lost. In the family of human beings, **God the Son, Jesus, became human in order to seek after human beings and reunite them with God the Father. In dying on the cross, Jesus took on shame and guilt and honored the Father by his perfect obedience.**

FRAME 5 ⟨ RESURRECTION

1 But Jesus did not remain dead. The Father honored Jesus' obedience by raising him from death to life. The word for this special rising to life is resurrection. We place a crown over the cross to represent the honor Jesus received in the resurrection.

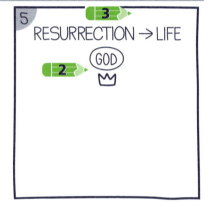

4 **When we choose to follow Jesus, his obedience is credited to us and our sin is forgiven. Jesus offers life, honor, and forgiveness to everyone who will follow him and return to God's family.** When we choose to follow him, Jesus sends the Holy Spirit to live inside of us to help us honor and obey God and honor others.

7 This is the main message of the Bible. What questions do you have?

1 Today there is a worldwide family connected to God and each other. Members of that family are working to bring harmony to the many broken relationships in our world.

4 Jesus offers two different invitations:

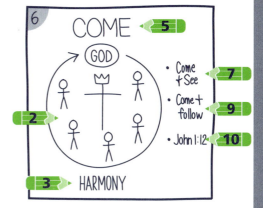

6 *Come and see:* Learn about Jesus through reading the Bible, praying, doing what he says, and spending time with his people. Become a sincere seeker after God.

8 *Come and follow:* Join Jesus and his family in bringing harmony to this broken world. John 1:12 tells us how: "Yet to all who did receive him, to those who believed in his name, he gave the right to become children of God" (NIV). To "receive" Jesus means to welcome him into your life as leader and teacher. To "believe in his name" means to trust in him deeply.

11 **Jesus is making these invitations today…**Are you ready to answer one of them or do you need some more time to think about it?

Invite people who want to commit to being sincere seekers to pray something like this:

▶ *"God, if you are real, please reveal yourself to me. If you do, I will make you the Leader of my life."*

Those desiring to become followers of Jesus could pray something like this:

▶ *"Father God, I have been living independently of you, but I want to come home to you. Thank you for sending Jesus to die for my sin. Please come into my life, take control, and fill me with your Holy Spirit. Thank you."*

For a different version of these diagrams that might be more effective with certain groups and an adaptation for Chinese, see crossingculturesbook.org/broken.

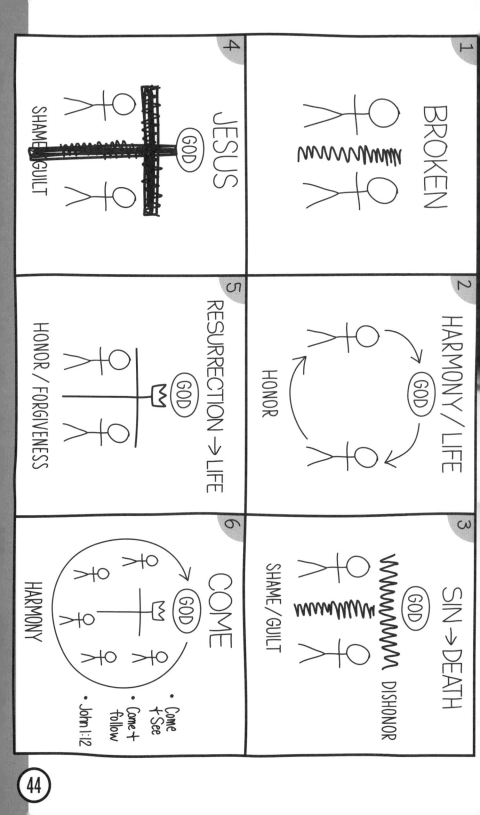

CHAPTER
3

GOD *the* HOLY SPIRIT

OPEN

- How did you put into practice what you learned from the Word last week?
- How did your practice of time alone with God go last week? Were you able to find a mature believer from your hometown or region and set up a time to meet and talk? Do you have any questions about the "Broken" diagrams?
- Take turns repeating the memory verse without looking at the guide.
- Pray briefly about what you shared and for your time in the Word.

 DIG IN

In the **Christian** faith, we believe in the one and only God who exists eternally in three Persons, the Father, the Son Jesus Christ, and the Holy Spirit. This is commonly referred to as the doctrine of the **Trinity**. The three Persons are distinct but they are one God and work in perfect unity and harmony. They appear throughout Scripture in different ways at different times, though often one Person is given more focus in particular books, such as Jesus in the four Gospels and the Holy Spirit in the book of Acts.

*1. What is your culture's understanding of the spiritual world?

2. Take a few minutes to read through the text. Mark words you do not know, items that impress you, and questions you have. Also mark everything you see that is related to the Spirit.

The Spirit of God would be familiar to a Jew during New Testament times. The Old Testament contains plenty of evidence that God moves and acts as the Spirit. A few examples include the Holy Spirit being present during the creation of the world (Genesis 1:2), the Holy Spirit providing power and rest to Moses and his people (Isaiah 63:11–14), and the fact that every prophet received God's messages through the Holy Spirit. The Old Testament also points to God's plan to introduce a new covenant to his people (Jeremiah 31:31–34). This refers to the future work of Jesus and, after Jesus' death and resurrection, the work of the Holy Spirit. So, when the disciples hear Jesus talk about the Spirit, they would have some sort of understanding of what this might mean.

JOHN 14:15–17, 25–26 (CEV) ¹⁵ Jesus said to his disciples: If you love me, you will do as I command. ¹⁶ Then I will ask the Father to send you the Holy Spirit who will help you and always be with you. ¹⁷ The Spirit will show you what is true. The people of this world cannot accept the Spirit, because they don't see or know him. But you know the Spirit, who is with you and will keep on living in you....²⁵ I have told you these things while I am still with you. ²⁶ But the Holy Spirit will come and help you, because the Father will send the Spirit to take my place. The Spirit will teach you everything and will remind you of what I said while I was with you.

JOHN 15:26–27 (NIV) ²⁶ When the Advocate[1] comes, whom I will send to you from the Father—the Spirit of truth who goes out from the Father—he will testify about me. ²⁷ And you also must testify, for you have been with me from the beginning.

JOHN 16:7–9, 12–15 (CEV) ⁷ But I tell you that I am going to do what is best for you. That is why I am going away. The Holy Spirit cannot come to help you until I leave. But after I am gone, I will send the Spirit to you. ⁸ The Spirit will come and show the people of this world the truth about sin and God's justice and the judgment.[2] ⁹ The Spirit will show them that they are wrong about sin, because they didn't have faith in me....¹² I have much more to say to you, but right now it would be more than you could understand. ¹³ The Spirit shows what is true and will come and guide you into the full truth. The Spirit doesn't speak on his own. He will tell you only what he has heard from me, and he will let you know what is going to happen. ¹⁴ The Spirit will bring glory to me by taking my message and telling it to you. ¹⁵ Everything that the Father has is mine. That is why I have said that the Spirit takes my message and tells it to you.

---

[1] Advocate here means "Defender." The Greek word referred to may mean comfort, encourage, or defend. Other translations of the word include "Comforter" and "Helper."

[2] Other translations use the word "convict" for this ministry of the Spirit. The Spirit convicts both non-believers and believers of sin.

▶ OBSERVE

3. Discuss any words that are unfamiliar and then let one person retell the text using their own words.

4. What impresses you from the text?

*5. Make a list of all the things a reader can learn about the character and work of the Holy Spirit from this passage.

   What is the Spirit's role with the Father and the Son, the believer, and those who do not yet believe?

▶ INTERPRET

6. What questions do you have? Answer the questions from the text and the context.

*7. If you had been one of those disciples in the room, how would you have felt when Jesus said that he was leaving?

   And when he promised to send the Holy Spirit?

*8. How would the Holy Spirit continue Jesus' ministry?

▶ APPLY

*9. How do you respond to the thought that the Holy Spirit will help you, always be with you, show you what is true, and guide you into full truth?

*10. Describe your experience of the Holy Spirit in your life now.

*11. Is there something you learned about the Holy Spirit's character or work from question five that you would like to understand or experience more of? Where might you need to be comforted or convicted?

RESPOND

Your discipline for the week is *lectio divina* ("divine reading"). The purpose of *lectio* is to approach a biblical text in such a way that opens you to listen to the Holy Spirit. *Lectio* allows you to meditate on Scripture and hear from God. For tips about meditating on scripture, see the box on p.64.

STEPS FOR GROUP *LECTIO DIVINA*

The group leader reads John 14:15–23 out loud slowly three times. During the **first reading**, all participants (including the leader) are to simply listen to the text with an open heart. Allow the Holy Spirit to impress certain words or phrases upon you. Feel free to write these down. Briefly, share with the group which words or phrases were impressed upon you. Resist the urge to analyze the words or phrases now.

During the **second reading**, ask the Holy Spirit to reveal to you why the word or phrase he impressed on you is significant. Briefly share with the group what the Holy Spirit might be revealing to you.

During the **final reading**, ask the Holy Spirit to help you know how the word or phrase can be applied to your life. Share this with the group and pray for help to respond as the Holy Spirit has led you.

Try *lectio divina* during some of your times with God this week using Scriptures about the Holy Spirit listed under "Dig Deeper". Follow the same steps listed above, but instead of sharing out loud, write down your responses in your devotional notebook.

HERE ARE A FEW TIPS FOR DISCERNING AND TESTING WHAT YOU HEAR WHILE DOING *LECTIO*:

GOD CAN SPEAK TO YOU THROUGH:

- ❍ a verse of Scripture
- ❍ a picture in your mind
- ❍ a word, phrase, or impression in your mind

TO TEST WHAT YOU HEAR

- ❍ Is it in agreement with the Word and the character of God?
- ❍ What do other, mature Christians think about it?
- ❍ Do you have the "peace of Christ" about it (Colossians 3:15)?

Read the memory verse together:

 JOHN 14:26 (NIV) But the Advocate, the Holy Spirit, whom the Father will send in my name, will teach you all things and will remind you of everything I have said to you.

Write these verses in your heart language here:

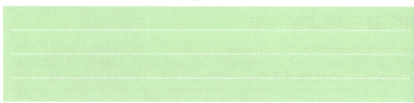

Memorize them in your heart language and English this week.

 ## DIG DEEPER

○ Learn more about the Holy Spirit through texts from Scripture. Study and/or do *lectio divina* with some of these passages this week. Write down any questions you have and discuss them with your *I-DIG* facilitator or coach over the next week.

⊙ **Ephesians 4:25–5:2** discusses ways we can grieve the Holy Spirit through sinful behavior or attitudes. **I Thessalonians 5:16–19** suggests actions that will help us not to quench (put out the fire of) the Spirit in our lives. Study these passages and ask God to show you if you are grieving or quenching the Spirit in any way.

⊙ **Acts 1:1–8** (being a witness through the power of the Spirit)

⊙ **Acts 2:1–13** (how the Holy Spirit came after Jesus departed)

⊙ **1 Corinthians 12:1–11** (the gifts of the Spirit)

⊙ **Galatians 5:16–26** (the fruit of the Spirit)

⊙ **Ephesians 5:15–21** (being continually filled with the Spirit)

○ Walk around your campus, city, or neighborhood and pray for the people who live there. Listen for the Spirit to guide you about how to pray. Also pray about what you hope to see God do in that place. This is called *prayer walking* and is a great way to invite the Holy Spirit to work in places you care about!

CHAPTER
4

IMAGE

BROKEN

OPEN

- How did you put into practice what you learned from the Word last week?
- How did your practice of time alone with God and *lectio divina* go last week?
- Take turns repeating the memory verse without looking at the guide.
- Pray briefly about what you shared and for your time in the Word.

 DIG IN

The Bible starts with very good news, then follows with very bad news, and ends with good news once again. The first good news and bad news occur in the first three chapters of the Bible, while the rest of the Bible is about God bringing people back to himself. In Genesis 1 we see that human beings are the climax of God's creation; he blesses them and provides food for them. In chapter 2 he provides companionship through marriage.

But it did not take long for people to turn from this loving God in disobedience, leading to the first **sin**. The first humans were created in God's image, but they quickly started a cycle of disobedience and distrust that lives on today in every single person.

*1. How do people in your culture view human nature?

2. Take a few minutes to read through the texts silently. Mark words you do not know and questions you have.

Genesis is the first book of the Bible. It covers the creation of the world and all that is in it, the great flood and Noah's ark, the Tower of Babel and the scattering of people throughout the world, and so much more. If time allows, read through all of Genesis 1–3. Otherwise, focus on the following verses.

GENESIS 1:26–31 (CEV)

26 God said, "Now we will make humans, and they will be like us. We will let them rule the fish, the birds, and all other living creatures." 27 So God created humans to be like himself; he made men and women.[1] 28 God gave them his blessing and said: "Have a lot of children! Fill the earth with people and bring it under your control. Rule over the fish in the ocean, the birds in the sky, and every animal on the earth. 29 I have provided all kinds of fruit and grain for you to eat. 30 And I have given the green plants as food for everything else that breathes. These will be food for animals, both wild and tame, and for birds." 31 God looked at what he had done. All of it was very good! Evening came and then morning—that was the sixth day.

GENESIS 2:24–25 (CEV)

24 That's why a man will leave his own father and mother. He marries a woman, and the two of them become like one person. 25 Although the man and his wife were both naked, they were not ashamed.

GENESIS 3:1–19 (CEV)

1 The snake was sneakier than any of the other wild animals that the Lord God had made. One day it came to the woman and asked, "Did God tell you not to eat fruit from any tree in the garden?"

2 The woman answered, "God said we could eat fruit from any tree in the garden, 3 except the one in the middle. He told us not to eat fruit from that tree or even to touch it. If we do, we will die."

4 "No, you won't!" the snake replied. 5 "God understands what will happen on the day you eat fruit from that tree. You will see what you have done, and you will know the difference between right and wrong, just as God does."

---

[1] The NIV translates Genesis 1:27 like this: "So God created man in his own image, in the image of God he created him; male and female he created them."

⁶ The woman stared at the fruit. It looked beautiful and tasty. She wanted the wisdom that it would give her, and she ate some of the fruit. Her husband was there with her, so she gave some to him, and he ate it too. ⁷ Right away they saw what they had done, and they realized they were naked. Then they sewed fig leaves together to make something to cover themselves.

⁸ Late in the afternoon a breeze began to blow, and the man and woman heard the Lord God walking in the garden. They were frightened and hid behind some trees.

⁹ The Lord called out to the man and asked, "Where are you?"

¹⁰ The man answered, "I was naked, and when I heard you walking through the garden, I was frightened and hid!"

¹¹ "How did you know you were naked?" God asked. "Did you eat any fruit from that tree in the middle of the garden?"

¹² "It was the woman you put here with me," the man said. "She gave me some of the fruit, and I ate it."

¹³ The Lord God then asked the woman, "What have you done?"

"The snake tricked me," she answered. "And I ate some of that fruit."

¹⁴ So the Lord God said to the snake: "Because of what you have done, you will be the only animal to suffer this curse—For as long as you live, you will crawl on your stomach and eat dirt. ¹⁵ You and this woman will hate each other; your descendants and hers will always be enemies. One of hers will strike you on the head, and you will strike him on the heel."[2]

¹⁶ Then the Lord said to the woman, "You will suffer terribly when you give birth. But you will still desire your husband, and he will rule over you."

---

[2] Genesis 3:15 refers to the ongoing warfare between human beings and Satan, the evil spirit who was working through the snake. The descendant of Eve who eventually struck Satan on the head was Jesus. See chapter eleven for information about Satan and spiritual warfare.

[17] The Lord said to the man, "You listened to your wife and ate fruit from that tree. And so, the ground will be under a curse because of what you did. As long as you live, you will have to struggle to grow enough food. [18] Your food will be plants, but the ground will produce thorns and thistles. [19] You will have to sweat to earn a living; you were made out of soil, and you will once again turn into soil."

GENESIS 3:23 (CEV)
[23] So the Lord God sent them out of the Garden of Eden, where they would have to work the ground from which the man had been made.

▶ OBSERVE

3. Discuss any words that are unfamiliar. Take turns retelling the story of the text in your own words.

*4. What was life like for Adam and Eve before and after they disobeyed God? Use the table below to record the differences.

BEFORE	AFTER

▶ INTERPRET

*5. Other translations of Genesis 1 say that human beings are "made in God's image". What does it mean that "God created humans to be like himself"?

How does God honor the human race by making us in his image?

6. Look at God's blessing and commands in Genesis 1:28–30. What does God want for people?

How does he treat them?

How would you feel if you were Adam or Eve?

*7. Look at the contrasts you found in question four. What has happened to the image of God in humans?

What do we learn about God from his response to what happens?

▶ APPLY

8. How do you feel about the idea that you are the climax of creation, made like God and blessed by him?

*9. How do you and your culture both reflect and not reflect the character of God?

*10. Behind every act of sin is a heart attitude and a belief that we know better than God. We don't trust him and decide to do things our own way, just as Eve and Adam did with the fruit. In what areas do you think or live as if you know better than God?

*11. How will you apply this lesson to your life here and now?

🦜 RESPOND

Like the first people, we turn from God often. Take time to **_confess_** _your sins_—with a friend or privately to God—and ask for forgiveness. Then offer those areas of your life to God, asking him to help you trust him and to change you.

We are also the best part of God's creation, made in his image for relationship with him. So your other discipline for the week is _practicing the presence of God._ Like Adam and Eve, we all tend to run away from God, whether consciously or unconsciously. Practicing the presence of God reminds us that he is with us always and helps us enjoy being his children. Here are some different ways you can practice God's presence. Try one or more of these this week.

- ⊙ Set an alarm on a watch or phone to go off each waking hour. Each time the alarm sounds, take a minute to remember that God is with you and that you live immersed in God's love.

- ⊙ Choose a repetitive activity during your day (such as walking to class; eating a meal; taking a sip of soda, water, or coffee) and couple this activity with the reminder of God's love and presence.

- ⊙ Wear a rubber band on your wrist or hand, and let the unusual feeling bring your mind back to God. Switch its position every day or so to keep the "odd" feeling.

Read the memory verse together:

▶ **PROVERBS 3:5–8 (NIV)** Trust in the Lord with all your heart and lean not on your own understanding; in all your ways submit to him, and he will make your paths straight. Do not be wise in your own eyes; fear the Lord and shun evil. This will bring health to your body and nourishment to your bones.

Eve and Adam leaned on their own understanding and were wise in their own eyes, and this led to sin. These verses remind us not to follow their example!

Write these verses in your heart language here:

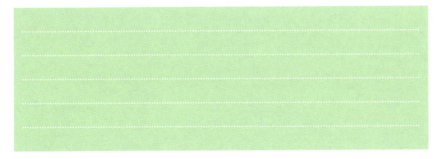

Memorize them in your heart language and English this week.

 DIG DEEPER

Study some of the passages below during your time alone with God this week:

- ● Read Genesis 1. What do you learn about the character of God?

- ● Read through Psalm 8. What do you learn about God? About people? Use this psalm as a prayer.

- ● Read Romans 1:20–25. What additional understanding do you get about how human beings fell into sin? What happens when people don't honor and thank God? What lies do people believe about God today? What do people serve today?

- ● Confession of sin is an important part of the Christian life because it keeps our relationship with God strong! Meditate on 1 John 1:5–9, which has a wonderful promise for those who confess their sins. See p. 64 for tips on how to meditate on Scripture.

- ● Psalm 51 is a prayer of confession that you can use as a template for your own prayer.

IMAGE

RESTORED

New Identity in Christ

OPEN

- How did you put into practice what you learned from the Word last week?
- How did your practice of **confession** go last week? How did practicing the presence of God go? How were your times alone with God?
- Take turns repeating the memory verse without looking at the guide.
- Pray briefly over what was shared and for your time in the Word.

DIG IN

It is not hard to notice the imperfection all around us, in government, injustice, human trafficking, businesses, and even our families. But God has a plan. When Jesus came, he proclaimed a new way of living that is under God's rule. This is possible through his death on the cross and his **resurrection**. It begins with our trust in him, which affects every decision and action in our lives.

*1. According to people in your culture, what is the best means to improve human beings and society?

2. Take a few minutes to read through the texts. Mark words you do not know, items that impress you, and questions you have. Also mark contrasts and parts of the passage that point to restoration and our new identity.

In the last chapter we learned we were made in God's perfect image. But this image was spoiled by disobedience and distrust, in other words by **sin**, which began a cycle that has persisted throughout history. God wants for each person to be restored to his perfect image. As a Father who loves us, he makes it possible, but we need to focus on him and follow him in obedience. A few weeks ago we read in Colossians 1 how Jesus died on the cross to reconcile us to God. In Colossians 2 Paul says that **Christians**, in their **baptisms**, share in Christ's death and resurrection. In baptism, which symbolizes and publicly speaks of our union with Christ, we rise to new spiritual life. Paul continues the thought in chapter 3.

COLOSSIANS 3:1–14 (NIV) *LM*

¹ Since, then, you have been raised with Christ, set your hearts on things above, where Christ is, seated at the right hand of God. ² Set your minds on things above, not on earthly things. ³ For you died, and your life is now hidden with Christ in God. ⁴ When Christ, who is your life, appears, then you also will appear with him in glory. ⁵ Put to death, therefore, whatever belongs to your earthly nature: sexual immorality, impurity, lust, evil desires and greed, which is idolatry. ⁶ Because of these, the wrath of God is coming. ⁷ You used to walk in these ways, in the life you once lived. ⁸ But now you must also rid yourselves of all such things as these: anger, rage, malice¹, slander², and filthy language from your lips. ⁹ Do not lie to each other, since you have taken off your old self with its practices ¹⁰ and have put on the new self, which is being renewed in knowledge in the image of its Creator. ¹¹ Here there is no Gentile or Jew, **circumcised** or uncircumcised, barbarian, Scythian, slave or free, but Christ is all, and is in all.³ ¹² Therefore, as God's chosen people, holy and dearly loved, clothe yourselves with compassion, kindness, humility, gentleness and patience. ¹³ Bear with each other and forgive one another if any of you has a grievance against someone. Forgive as the Lord forgave you. ¹⁴ And over all these virtues put on love, which binds them all together in perfect unity.

[handwritten annotations: "đời sống ju'o (lsạch", "lộg tham", "tham lam", "lộg trắc ản", "Khiêm tốn", "complaint", "good things", "thống I"]

---

¹ *Malice* is the desire to harm other people or do bad things.
² *Slander* is saying false and harmful things about another person.
³ *Gentiles* were non-Jews. The Jews were the people God chose to be the family of Jesus. Jews **circumcised** male babies and Gentiles did not, so being circumcised was a mark of being **Jewish**. *Barbarians* were uncivilized people; *Scythians* were considered particularly uncivilized. In this verse Paul is saying that religious, racial, and cultural distinctions are no longer our primary identity as we are renewed in the image of God by living our lives with Jesus.

▶ OBSERVE

3. Retell the text using your own words.

*4. What impresses you from the text?

▶ INTERPRET

5. What questions do you have? Answer the questions from the text and the context.

*6. Try to summarize the passage in one sentence. What is the main point?

*7. What things need to be taken off and put on?

   How is this new life appropriate for someone restored in the image of God?

▶ APPLY

It is common for Christians to view themselves as saved sinners rather than as children of God. When we see ourselves as saved sinners, our primary identity is still our old selves and we tend to obey out of guilt, shame, or obligation. But if we see ourselves as children of God who still occasionally sin, we obey out of love and gratitude to our Father. True transformation occurs as we focus on our identity as dearly loved children.

*8. Look at your lists from question seven. What things will be hardest for you to take off or put on?

*9. How can setting your mind on Christ and remembering that you are a dearly loved child of the Father help you take off the old and put on the new?

10. For people who decide to follow Jesus wholeheartedly, being baptized is an important step to take. See the box below titled "Special Notes on Baptism Today." What commitments did you make at your baptism that you need to be faithful to now? If you have not been baptized, share with your group the reason why and prayerfully consider taking that step.

*11. How will you apply what you have learned in this chapter to your life here and now?

   How would this apply to your life back home?

SPECIAL NOTES ON BAPTISM TODAY

Today various churches have different practices concerning *how* people are baptized: sprinkling, pouring, full immersion or plunging underwater. They also differ in *who* should be baptized. Some baptize babies as a sign that God gave them to Christian parents and to Christ's people, who promise to teach them to follow Christ. Others reserve baptism for people who consciously choose to follow Jesus and dedicate babies to God instead of baptizing them.

Sometimes new international believers have postponed baptism out of concern for how it would impact their family and friends. Not wanting to have relationships with family and friends cut off so completely that there would be no way to influence them for Jesus, they have waited to be baptized until they could show their families by their lives that following Jesus brings about good changes. This kind of decision may be needed in a small number of cases. If you have not been baptized yet, ask God to lead you about the timing.

For a definition and biblical references to baptism, please see "Baptism" in the "Word and Concept List."

RESPOND

How we think greatly influences how we live, so it is important to think thoughts that agree with God, both about who God is and who we are. This is one reason we memorize and meditate on Scripture. This week, **during your time alone with God, choose one or two of the statements below each day**, look up the verse, and meditate on what this part of your new identity means to you. See below for tips on how to meditate on Scripture. Reading this list aloud is also helpful to remind yourself of these truths.

In Christ, I am:

- chosen and dearly loved — Colossians 3:12
- a child of God — John 1:12
- a new creature, a new creation — 2 Corinthians 5:17
- a royal priest — 1 Peter 2:9
- an ambassador for Christ — 2 Corinthians 5:20
- a light for the world — Matthew 5:14
- able to do all things through Christ — Philippians 4:13
- more than a conqueror — Romans 8:37–39
- a member of God's family — Ephesians 4:4
- a friend of Jesus — John 15:14–15

▶ TIPS FOR MEDITATING ON SCRIPTURE ◀

Prayerfully hold the verses in your mind, thinking about them slowly and carefully. The idea is that of a cow chewing its cud very slowly. Do whatever you can to spiritually take in and "digest" the Scripture. The Bible has been compared to milk, meat, and honey; meditating enables us to take in and benefit from this spiritual food. As you meditate, you might want to ask yourself and God questions about the verses. You could also write them in your own words, draw a picture to illustrate them, or read them in more than one translation. Record any thoughts that come to you in your devotional notebook.

Read the memory verse together:

▶ **2 CORINTHIANS 5:17–18 (CEV)** Anyone who belongs to Christ is a new person. The past is forgotten, and everything is new. God has done it all! He sent Christ to make peace between himself and us, and he has given us the work of making peace between himself and others.

Write these verses in your heart language here:

Memorize them in your heart language and English this week.

DIG DEEPER

- **Ephesians 4:20–5:2** is another list of "put off/put on" commands. Study these verses and ask God to show you what additional behaviors you might need to put off or put on.

- **Colossians 3:13** commands us to forgive people who have hurt us. Prayerfully make a list of people you need to forgive and start asking for God's help to do so. Get others to pray for and with you about this if needed. See "Tool F: Forgiveness" on p.79.

- Read *Victory Over the Darkness: Realizing the Power of Your Identity in Christ* by Neil T. Anderson (Regal Books).

See the Freedom in Christ Ministries website for more identity statements: *www.ficm.org/handy-links/#!/who-i-am-in-christ* (These identity statements and Anderson's book will help you become firmly grounded in your identity as a child of God.)

CHAPTER
6

TRUST &
FREEDOM

OPEN

- How did you put into practice what you learned from the Word last week?
- How did your practice of time alone with God and meditation on the identity statements go last week?
- Take turns repeating the memory verse without looking at the guide.
- Pray briefly about what you shared and for your time in the Word.

DIG IN

All humans serve some*thing* or some*one*, such as success, money, power, drugs or alcohol, sex, religious teachers, spiritual beings, family members, or bosses. The things we serve are also the things we trust, believing that they will help us survive or bring us a better life. In Matthew 6, Jesus says we can only have one master.

*1.   In your country, what things do people trust or worship the most?

*2.   Take a few minutes to read through the text silently. Mark words you do not know and questions you have. Look for repetition, commands, questions, and word pictures.

Matthew 5–7 contains Jesus' "Sermon on the Mount." These are some of Jesus' first words to his **disciples**. He has a lot to say to them about how to live their lives. One of the topics Jesus addresses is worry.

During the time of Jesus, people lived simple lifestyles. Food and clothes were basic necessities just as they are now, but people were even more dependent on the weather than we are today for their food and many other resources. For example, if there was drought, extreme rain, fire, or hail, crops could be ruined. It was easy to worry.

MATTHEW 6:24–34 (NIV)

²⁴ No one can serve two masters. Either you will hate the one and love the other, or you will be devoted to the one and despise the other. You cannot serve both God and money. ²⁵ Therefore I tell you, do not worry about your life, what you will eat or drink; or about your body, what you will wear. Is not life more than food, and the body more than clothes? ²⁶ Look at the birds of the air; they do not sow or reap or store away in barns, and yet your heavenly Father feeds them. Are you not much more valuable than they? ²⁷ Can any one of you by worrying add a single hour to your life? ²⁸ And why do you worry about clothes? See how the flowers of the field grow. They do not labor or spin. ²⁹ Yet I tell you that not even Solomon[1] in all his splendor was dressed like one of these. ³⁰ If that is how God clothes the grass of the field, which is here today and tomorrow is thrown into the fire, will he not much more clothe you—you of little faith? ³¹ So do not worry, saying, "What shall we eat?" or "What shall we drink?" or "What shall we wear?" ³² For the pagans run after all these things, and your heavenly Father knows that you need them. ³³ But seek first his **kingdom** and his **righteousness**, and all these things will be given to you as well. ³⁴ Therefore do not worry about tomorrow, for tomorrow will worry about itself. Each day has enough trouble of its own.

---

[1] Solomon was King David's son and the wealthiest and wisest man in the Bible (1 Kings 3:7–14).

▶ OBSERVE

3. Discuss any words that are unfamiliar.

    *What are the main themes or ideas that you observed?

4. Take turns retelling the text using your own words.

▶ INTERPRET

5. What questions do you have? Answer the questions from the text and the context.

6. What specific issues of life cause worry in this passage?

    How does that compare to today?

*7. In the midst of the commands, questions, and word pictures in these verses there is a promise (v. 33). What would this verse have meant to the original readers?

▶ APPLY

*8. What causes the most worry in your life? Why?

    How does this passage speak into that area of your life?

*9. In the margin, write down the things in your life that you tend to trust more than God. Share with your group members what you wrote. Spend a few minutes considering how giving up control of these things and allowing your heavenly Father to be Lord over them could bring freedom.

*10. Take turns praying and asking God to help you surrender the things you want control over. Pay attention to the Holy Spirit during this time and follow his leading.

    What practices might the Holy Spirit be leading you to as a result of surrender (for example, thanksgiving or forgiveness)?

RESPOND

After six days of creating the world, God rested on the seventh day. He commands us to do the same as a way to honor him. Sabbath is a gift from God to help us both rest and learn to trust him. It is more than a day off to leisurely do as we please; it is an entire day of focused time given to resting, being with God, and enjoying family. Sabbath is an excellent way to remind ourselves that God is in control, not us. In choosing to rest, we are surrendering our time to him and trusting that he will take care of the things we are not doing that day (such as work, homework, chores, emails and errands).

Practice taking a Sabbath this week. Choose a 24-hour period of time in the next week as your Sabbath, and use that time to sleep as much as you need to, to read your Bible, to pray, to read books by **Christian** authors, to journal, to spend quality time with a spouse or family member, or to do relaxing activities you enjoy that honor God. This is not a time to host a party, do your laundry, run your errands, or escape into technology. Focus on rest and time with God. If it is helpful, keep notes about your Sabbath and share next week from those notes about the things that were both enjoyable and difficult.

Read the memory verse together:

 MATTHEW 6:33 (NIV) But seek first his kingdom and his righteousness, and all these things will be given to you as well.

Write these verses in your heart language here:

Memorize them in your heart language and English this week.

 **DIG DEEPER**

Readings for now and later:

- ○ Read through the entire Sermon on the Mount (Matthew 5–7) to see how Jesus describes what "seeking first the kingdom" looks like. Read through a few sections each day during your time alone with God.

- ○ Matthew 6:7–13 (the Lord's Prayer) and 7:24–29 deal with freedom and lordship.

- ○ Watch the old movie *Chariots of Fire* to see how God honored someone who honored him according to 2 Samuel 2:30b.

- ○ The InterVarsity Press booklet *My Heart—Christ's Home* by Robert Boyd Munger challenges us to make Jesus Lord of each aspect of our lives.

- ○ *Celebration of Discipline: The Path to Spiritual Growth* by Richard J. Foster (HarperSanFrancisco) is a wonderful book to learn how deeply God can grow us through spiritual disciplines.

- ○ *Sabbath Keeping: Finding Freedom in the Rhythms of Rest* by Lynne Baab (InterVarsity Press) will help you understand the Sabbath more.

- ○ *Invitation to Solitude and Silence: Experiencing God's Transforming Presence* by Ruth Haley Barton (InterVarsity Press) will help you learn how to be in God's presence in solitude and silence.

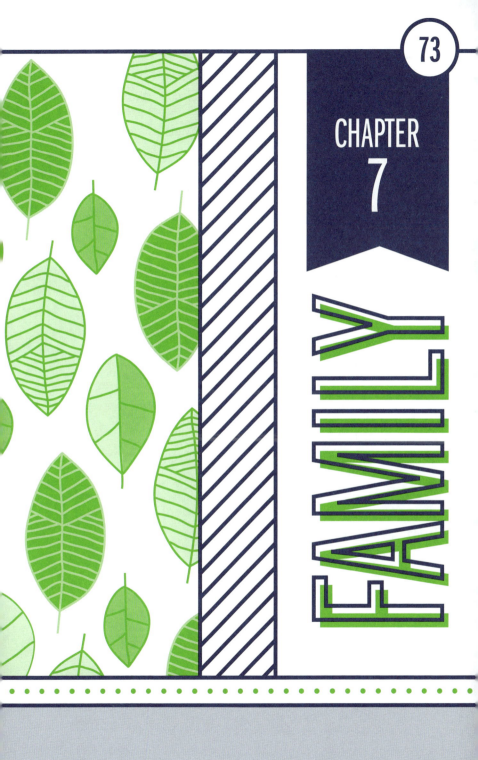

CHAPTER
7

FAMILY

OPEN

- How did you put into practice what you learned from the Word last week?
- How did your time alone with God and your practice of the Sabbath go last week?
- Take turns repeating the memory verse without looking at the guide.
- Pray briefly over what was shared and for your time in the Word.

 DIG IN

Because most people are closer to their own family than they are to anyone else in their lives, family is often a great source of joy, support, and love. But family can also be a source of pain and betrayal. The more you read the Bible, the more you will see that God wants what is best for us. He wants us to get the most out of our lives, starting with a relationship with him. That relationship then affects every other part of our lives, including family. He wants us to have excellent and healthy relationships with those closest to us.

*1. What is the most important family relationship (husband-wife, mother-son, etc.) in your culture?

What would a healthy example of this relationship look like?

How could this relationship be difficult?

*2. Take a few minutes to read through the texts silently. Mark words you do not know, items that impress you and questions you have. Also look for repeated words and ideas.

Chapters 4–6 of Paul's letter to the Ephesian __Christians__ focus on how we are to live as people of light, as people who are part of God's kingdom. Much is said about staying away from sin and foolish talk, and embracing honesty and a Spirit-filled life. Part of living this life filled with the Spirit is honoring Christ by putting others first. Paul then addresses various relationships. He chooses to emphasize marriage.

EPHESIANS 5:21–6:4 (CEV)

[21] Honor Christ and put others first. [22] A wife should put her husband first, as she does the Lord. [23] A husband is the head of his wife, as Christ is the head and the Savior of the church, which is his own body. [24] Wives should always put their husbands first, as the church puts Christ first. [25] A husband should love his wife as much as Christ loved the church and gave his life for it. [26] He made the church holy by the power of his word, and he made it pure by washing it with water. [27] Christ did this, so that he would have a glorious and holy church, without faults or spots or wrinkles or any other flaws. [28] In the same way, a husband should love his wife as much as he loves himself. A husband who loves his wife shows that he loves himself. [29] None of us hate our own bodies. We provide for them and take good care of them, just as Christ does for the church, [30] because we are each part of his body. [31] As the Scriptures say, "A man leaves his father and mother to get married, and he becomes like one person with his wife."[1] [32] This is a great mystery, but I understand it to mean Christ and his church. [33] So each husband should love his wife as much as he loves himself, and each wife should respect her husband.

[1] Children, you belong to the Lord, and you do the right thing when you obey your parents. The first commandment with a promise says, [2] "Obey your father and your mother, [3] and you will have a long and happy life."[2] [4] Parents, don't be hard on your children. Raise them properly. Teach them and instruct them about the Lord.

---

[1] Genesis 2:24
[2] Exodus 20:12

▶ OBSERVE

*3.   Retell the text using your own words.

4.   What impresses you from the text?

▶ INTERPRET

*5.   Why does Paul use Jesus and the church to teach husbands and wives how to treat each other? Compare the two relationships.

6.   How would these commands have challenged those who first heard or read them?

▶ APPLY

Verse 21 can also be translated, "Submit to one another out of reverence for Christ" (NIV). The sections on marriage, parents and children, and masters and slaves that follow are all outworkings of this command.

*7.   The CEV translates verse 21 as "Honor Christ and put others first." Who do you know who models this in your culture?

Where do you need to put this into practice in your family life?

8.   When you look at your marriage or your parents' marriage, how does it compare to what is described in this passage?

How would your life be different if your marriage or your parents' marriage were more like this?

*9.   What from this passage can you start applying to your marriage this week? If you are not married, what does God want to say to you about dating and marriage?

*10.   As a parent and/or child, how can you apply the last few verses?

11.   Are there other family relationships you need to submit to God? Is there anyone you need to **forgive**[3]?

---

[3] See "Tool F: Forgiveness" on p.79 to learn more.

RESPOND

Intercession is praying for other people. This week we will do this by praying for specific family members and relationships. Make a short list of family members to pray for, and ask God to lead you and teach you how to pray for them. Paul's prayers for the Ephesians (Ephesians 1:17–19a and Ephesians 3:17b–19) are good places to begin.

As you pray for family members, you may realize that you need to forgive a family member or ask for forgiveness. Ask God to help. If this is difficult, meet with a Christian friend, staff worker, or pastor to pray together about this issue. Forgiving and seeking forgiveness take courage, but the Holy Spirit will direct and help us if we sincerely desire to obey God in these areas. See the tool on forgiveness directly following this chapter.

Read the memory verse together:

 EPHESIANS 5:21 (NIV) Submit to one another out of reverence for Christ.

Write it in your heart language here:

Memorize it in your heart language and English this week.

🔖 DIG DEEPER

Ephesians 4 and **5** contain many general commands about relationships that also apply to family life. Read and meditate on these chapters section-by-section during your time alone with God this week.

- ○ Ephesians 4:26–27 is especially important. Meditate on these two verses and ask God to help you to not hold on to anger overnight.

- ○ Meditate on Colossians 3:15–21, which contains similar commands from Paul.

- ○ What about dating or marrying non-Christians? See 2 Corinthians 6:14–18.

- ○ What if I'm married to a non-Christian? See 1 Peter 3:1–4 and 1 Corinthians 7:12–16.

- ○ If you were married to or dating a non-Christian before you became a Christian, start praying for them immediately! God can use you to draw them to him.

- ○ For more on honoring parents, compare Exodus 20:12 with Ephesians 6:1–3.

- ○ When obeying God and obeying parents conflict, we must obey God. See Acts 5:29.

- ○ *Following Jesus Without Dishonoring Your Parents* by Jeanette Yep, Peter Cha, Paul Tokunaga, Greg Jao, and Susan Cho Van Riesen (InterVarsity Press) contains a chapter on what it means to "honor" and "obey" that can help you sort through some of these family issues.

- ○ *Are You Waiting for "The One"? Cultivating Realistic, Positive Expectations for Christian Marriage* by Margaret Kim Peterson and Dwight N. Peterson (InterVarsity Press) will help you develop realistic expectations for marriage.

- ○ *As for Me and My House: Crafting Your Marriage to Last* by Walter Wangerin Jr. (Thomas Nelson) is a helpful book on marriage.

- ○ *Sex and Dating: Questions You Wish You Had Answers To* by Mindy Meier (InterVarsity Press) addresses these topics helpfully.

- ○ Matthew 19:10–12 implies that some people have been given a gift of singleness. If you are single, consider praying about whether you should marry. Others may feel led to pray for the person who will one day become their spouse.

- ○ If you're married, pray for your spouse.

FORGIVENESS

WHAT IS FORGIVENESS?

It is canceling the debt of a person who has wronged us while taking on the cost of repayment ourselves. It includes:

- acknowledging what really happened: *hurting*
- sending away our emotional reaction to what happened
- canceling the punishment we want to give the person
- paying the cost ourselves by going through the emotional work needed for our own healing and eventual reconciliation

Restored friendship can/should only occur if the other person is ready and trustworthy.

WHY FORGIVE?

- To obey God and follow Jesus' example
- To prevent emotional and even physical torment and allow healing into our lives
- To prevent hurt to other people
- To open up the possibility of restored relationship with the person
- To remain in strong relationship with God

WHY CAN IT BE SO HARD TO FORGIVE OR GIVE GRACE AND PATIENCE TO OTHERS?

- We have not experienced forgiveness ourselves on the human level and don't have models.
- Deep down, we want to earn God's grace and we believe that others should earn ours.
- We're used to relationships based on obligation.
- We haven't allowed ourselves to truly receive and experience the gift of God's grace.
- We're not patient and forgiving of ourselves.

PRACTICAL STEPS IN FORGIVING:

- Ask for the Holy Spirit's help.
- Allow yourself to feel what you're feeling (maybe grief, hurt, etc.).
- Ask God to make you willing to forgive even as you are filled with anger and hate. Do not let the sun go down on your anger without asking for the grace to forgive (Ephesians 4:26–27).
- Think about the example of Jesus and other Christians (see Luke 23:33–34 and Acts 7:59–60).
- Ask God to help you see the other person with his eyes and understand them better.
- State your intention to forgive as an act of the will and ask God to bring your emotions along.
- Have a special prayer time with a Christian friend about forgiveness. Ask God for daily grace to continue in an attitude of forgiveness.

EXPRESSING FORGIVENESS CROSS-CULTURALLY:

Indirect cultures deal with conflict indirectly, sometimes using a mediator or communicating through stories. Expressing forgiveness to a person from an indirect culture may therefore need to be done indirectly. Consult Duane Elmer's *Cross-Cultural Conflict* (InterVarsity Press) for more insights.

Note: Some of these ideas come from the InterVarsity Press booklet *Forgiveness* by Dan Hamilton and Lewis Smedes's book *Forgive and Forget: Healing the Hurts We Don't Deserve* (HarperOne).

CHAPTER
8

The CHURCH

OPEN

- How did you put into practice what you learned from the Word last week?

- How did your practice of time alone with God and **intercession** for family members go last week? Did you have a chance to make a forgiveness list?

- Take turns repeating the memory verse without looking at the guide.

- Pray briefly about what you shared and for your time in the Word.

 DIG IN

Church is not a *place people go* but a Christian *community to which people belong*. Church has the potential to provide great encouragement, learning, spiritual growth, encounters with the Holy Spirit, and care for both Christians and those who are seeking to know more about Christ.

*1. Describe your experience with church so far, both here in this country and in your home country (if you have been part of a church there).

What do you appreciate about your church community? What is difficult?

2. Take a few minutes to read through the text silently. Mark words you do not know, items that impress you and questions you have. *Also look for verbs and other words that describe this first church.

The book of Acts begins with Jesus' final words to his followers to wait for the Holy Spirit to come and his ascension[1] into heaven. After the Holy Spirit comes in a powerful way (Acts 2:1–13), the believers, led by Simon Peter, begin the first church. Remembering what Jesus taught them and following the Holy Spirit, this community takes form.

In Acts 2:41, "his message" refers to Peter's words to the crowd about the prophecy of the Holy Spirit's coming and the explanation of Jesus' purpose and true identity as Lord. His hearers wanted to know what they should do in response, and Peter urged them to repent, be baptized, and expect to receive the Holy Spirit (see Acts 2:14–40).

---
[1] *Ascension* is a special word used to describe Jesus' return to be with his Father.

ACTS 2:41–47 (NIV)

[41] Those who accepted his message were baptized, and about three thousand were added to their number that day. [42] They devoted themselves to the apostles' teaching and to fellowship, to the breaking of bread[2] and to prayer. [43] Everyone was filled with awe at the many wonders and signs performed by the apostles. [44] All the believers were together and had everything in common. [45] They sold property and possessions to give to anyone who had need. [46] Every day they continued to meet together in the temple courts. They broke bread in their homes and ate together with glad and sincere hearts, [47] praising God and enjoying the favor of all the people. And the Lord added to their number daily those who were being saved.

▶ OBSERVE

*3.   Discuss any words that are unfamiliar. Retell the story of the text using your own words.

4.   What impresses you from the text?

▶ INTERPRET

5.   What questions do you have? Answer the questions from the text and the context.

*6.   How would you describe this community?

      What activities did this first church engage in?

      What were the results?

7.   What challenges would being part of this first church have presented?

      What lifestyle changes would have been required for the individuals involved?

---

[2] The "breaking of bread" refers to communion, the Lord's Supper.

▶ APPLY

8. Being part of a church and meeting regularly with other Christians who are part of it as well (through church services, a small group or a Bible study) is really important to stay grounded in your faith and to grow spiritually. Where do you go to church now?

   In light of this passage, how is your current church or community really being and doing what the church is supposed to be and do? What changes might you need to pray for?

*9. If you needed to start a simple church, what would be the essential components, based on this passage?

   How could you put into practice some of your experience in this I-DIG group and in other similar groups?

*10. Church in your home country might be very different than your experience here in the U.S. has been. For example, there might be big differences in the worship styles, teaching styles, and physical buildings of each church. What do you need to do to prepare your heart before returning home to a different church setting? If you are not returning home soon, how do you feel you need to respond to this passage? Share out loud small or big things that come to mind and pray for one other.

RESPOND

Some people worship God in large churches with hundreds or thousands of people. Other people worship God in small groups (sometimes called a "house church") that often have fewer than twenty-five other worshipers. Think about your home country or the country where you will live next. What size and type of church will you most likely join? Will it be large or will it be a small group of people meeting together for Bible study and prayer? It is important to learn about the many dynamics of different church communities. Remember that the style of worship and teaching are not the important factors when considering a church! Instead, finding a church that values true biblical teaching, serving and loving the Christian and non-Christian communities alike, and worshiping God from the heart are the important factors.

THIS WEEK:

Research churches in your current city and visit ones that resemble churches you might be part of in the future. It would be ideal to visit a church that worships in your heart language. Ask questions of participants in the church, such as, "How did this group form?" or "What does the leadership look like here?" or "How are the worshipers needed to carry out the vision of the church?" (It's fine if it takes you an additional week or two to get to a different church. But at least make a plan this week for when you'll go, and put it on your calendar!)

Read the memory verse together:

 EPHESIANS 4:2–3 (NIV) Be completely humble and gentle; be patient, bearing with one another in love. Make every effort to keep the unity of the Spirit through the bond of peace.

Write these verses in your heart language here:

Memorize them in your heart language and English this week.

 **DIG DEEPER**

There are many opportunities to deepen our understanding and experience of church. Consider the following list and choose, as a group or as individuals, one or more of the suggestions to try. You can study the Scriptures in bold during your times alone with God and pick one of the suggested actions as an application.

- ❍ Study or meditate on these texts about giving: **Matthew 6:1–4; Mark 12:41–44; 2 Corinthians 9:7–11; Philippians 4:10–19.**

- ❍ Begin giving financially to your church or give a special gift of money to a Christian missionary or other Christian work you know about.

- ❍ Read **Ephesians 2:11–22** and **Romans 12:3–16**. What do we learn about the church from these texts?

- ❍ Ephesians 2 talks about how people from different racial and cultural backgrounds are all one in Christ. Try visiting a church that is very culturally different from the one you usually attend. What do you learn about church from this experience?

- ❍ Give some extra time to serving in your church or to serving others with your church family.

CHAPTER
9

SALT & LIGHT

OPEN

- How did you put into practice what you learned from the Word last week?

- How did your practice of time alone with God and your visit to a church similar to those you might be part of back home go last week? Did you try any of the other suggestions in last week's "Dig Deeper"?

- Take turns repeating the memory verse without looking at the guide.

- Pray briefly about what you shared and for your time in the Word.

 DIG IN

In Genesis 12, God initiates with Abraham. He says, "I will make you into a great nation, and I will bless you…and all peoples on earth will be blessed through you" (Genesis 12:2–3b NIV). God loves blessing his children, but this blessing is not meant to be kept to ourselves. As we are blessed, we are to bless others.

Similarly, when Jesus called his **disciples**, he called them first to be with him and then to do deeds of love and share the good news with others. God's priority is for all to know him. And as we grow closer to God and follow him, we also need to love and share the good news with others and be salt and light in our world. We will learn what salt and light means in today's study.

*1. How do people from your culture respond to those who share their religious beliefs with others?

*2. Take a few minutes to read through the texts silently. Mark words you do not know, items that impress you and questions you have.

_____

_____

_____

_____

As we learned in chapter six, Matthew 5–7 contains Jesus' "Sermon on the Mount." These are some of Jesus' first words to his disciples. Verses 11 and 12 of Matthew 5 are the last two verses of the "Beatitudes," nine statements about who is truly blessed. The term beatitude comes from the Latin word for "blessed." The word blessed (see the NIV translation of Matthew 5:11) refers to the eternal well-being and spiritual joy of God's children. The verses from Matthew 9 that we will study contain words Jesus spoke just before he chose his twelve special disciples.

MATTHEW 5:11–16 (CEV)

[11] God will bless you when people insult you, mistreat you, and tell all kinds of evil lies about you because of me. [12] Be happy and excited! You will have a great reward in heaven. People did these same things to the prophets who lived long ago. [13] You are like salt for everyone on earth. But if salt no longer tastes like salt, how can it make food salty? All it is good for is to be thrown out and walked on. [14] You are like light for the whole world. A city built on top of a hill cannot be hidden, [15] and no one would light a lamp and put it under a clay pot. A lamp is placed on a lampstand, where it can give light to everyone in the house. [16] Make your light shine, so that others will see the good that you do and will praise your Father in heaven.

MATTHEW 9:35–38 (NIV)

[35] Jesus went through all the towns and villages, teaching in their synagogues, proclaiming the good news of the kingdom and healing every disease and sickness. [36] When he saw the crowds, he had compassion on them, because they were harassed and helpless, like sheep without a shepherd. [37] Then he said to his disciples, "The harvest is plentiful but the workers are few. [38] Ask the Lord of the harvest, therefore, to send out workers into his harvest field."

▶ OBSERVE

*3.   Discuss any words that are unfamiliar. Retell the texts with your own words.

4.   What impresses you from the texts?

▶ INTERPRET

*5.   What do the pictures of light and salt teach us about the role that followers of Jesus are supposed to have in the world?

*6.   How are followers of Jesus to respond to persecution? Why?

*7.   Look at the Matthew 9 passage. How did Jesus' compassion impact what he did and what he wanted his disciples to do?

How do these verses create a sense of urgency?

▶ APPLY

*8.   What mistreatment or persecution have you received because of following Jesus?

What persecution might you experience when (or if) you return home?

How does this passage challenge and encourage you?

9.   How are people who don't know Jesus like sheep without a shepherd?

10.   Think about people who don't know Jesus from your home country or region. What is a culturally appropriate way to share the gospel with them?

*11.   Where or with whom do you need to be light and salt starting today? Talk about practical ways you can apply this lesson this coming week (such as initiating a friendship, doing something good for someone or sharing your testimony with a particular person). Start by praying for a non-Christian friend and for more workers, especially for the harvest back home.

🫖 RESPOND

An essential part of being salt and light is *sharing your testimony*. We can share formally before a large group or casually in a one-on-one conversation. Either way, the more prepared we are, the better. Take time this week to prepare a three-to-five-minute testimony that you will share with others. Use the outline below to help. Remember that your testimony should be appropriate for your audience. Avoid words that only Christians understand and highlight parts of your testimony that might appeal most to your listeners:

- ⊙ Briefly describe your life before you followed Jesus.
- ⊙ What events/lessons/conversations/people led to your conversion?
- ⊙ Describe how you decided to trust and commit to Jesus.
- ⊙ How has your life changed since your decision? In what ways do you have hope and purpose for the future?
- ⊙ End with an encouragement or challenge for your audience.

Remember, your testimony is both about *telling your story* and *influencing your audience*. Say only what you need to say and tell it in a way that is engaging without exaggerating or bending the truth. Be real. Practice with one another next week and start asking God who you could share your testimony with. Pray for those people and for an opportunity.

Read the memory verse together:

▶ **MATTHEW 5:14–16 (CEV)** You are like light for the whole world. A city built on top of a hill cannot be hidden, and no one would light a lamp and put it under a clay pot. A lamp is placed on a lampstand, where it can give light to everyone in the house. Make your light shine, so that others will see the good that you do and will praise your Father in heaven.

Write the memory verses in your heart language or another translation here:

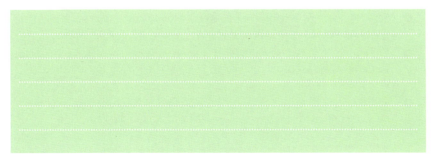

Memorize them in your heart language and English this week.

DIG DEEPER

- Read **Acts 17:16–34, John 3:1–17,** and **John 4:1–42**. What do you learn about evangelism from Paul and Jesus? You might need to take more than one day to study each of these passages because there is so much to learn from them!

- Read Paul's story of his conversion in Acts 26:1–32 and use the structure and content as a model in writing out your own story.

- For some good online models of testimonies, go to *www.the315project.com*. Under "Connect with Us" at the bottom of the page, click on the last item, "Vimeo."

- Consider leading some non-Christian friends through the I-GIG studies— you can find them at *tiny.cc/igig*.

- *Out of the Saltshaker & into the World* by Rebecca Manley Pippert (InterVarsity Press) is a helpful book on evangelism.

- The "Broken" diagrams on p.39 explain the gospel in ways that group-oriented people understand well. If you haven't learned how to use these diagrams, do so this week. Pray and consider whom you could share them with soon.

- Study additional gospel presentations such as "God's Good News," which can be found on pp.60–61 of InterVarsity's *I-GIG* guide (*tiny.cc/igig*).

- *Radical: Taking Back Your Faith from the American Dream* by David Platt (Multnomah) is a good example of critiquing American Christian culture in the area of being salt and light.

- Attend the triennial Urbana Student Missions Conference or go to *www.urbana.org* to learn more about global missions.

- Show hospitality by opening your home to someone. Pray about how you can be salt and light among your neighbors.

- Serve the poor by feeding the homeless, tutoring less-resourced children, or giving money to organizations that help the poor around the world.

- Get into the habit of giving to those around you who are in need. This helps you love others practically and keeps you from becoming too attached to your possessions.

- Interview one or more Christians in the profession you have chosen or are pursuing and ask them how they are salt and light in the workplace.

CHAPTER 10

TEMPTATION and SUFFERING

OPEN

- How did you put into practice what you learned from the Word last week?

- How did your practice of time alone with God and writing your testimony go last week? Let one person share his or her three-to-five-minute testimony, and continue with others in the next few weeks.

- Take turns repeating the memory verse without looking at the guide.

- Pray briefly about what you shared and for your time in the Word.

DIG IN

Christians throughout history and throughout the world have experienced trials, temptation, and suffering for their faith. We can think about biblical characters, martyrs[1] from the past and present, missionaries around the world, and followers of Jesus who currently experience suffering in their day-to-day life. Throughout Scripture we see that trials are a normal part of the life of believers. However, this topic is often overlooked by North American Christians.

*1. Where are people suffering for their faith in the world today?

What do you think gives them the strength to keep going?

*2. Take a few minutes to read through the text silently. Mark words you do not know, questions you have and commands.

James is writing to the Jewish Christians in Palestine regarding the way they had been treated by the rich. Those who were not rich were experiencing oppression and poverty. They were caught on the wrong side of social tensions, and their land was being taken from them. James tells these Christians how to respond to these trials.

---

[1] The original meaning of martyr is "witness." Christian martyrs point others to Christ because of their willingness to die for him.

JAMES 1:2–17 (NIV)

[2] Consider it pure joy, my brothers and sisters, whenever you face trials[2] of many kinds, [3] because you know that the testing of your faith produces perseverance. [4] Let perseverance finish its work so that you may be mature and complete, not lacking anything. [5] If any of you lacks wisdom, you should ask God, who gives generously to all without finding fault, and it will be given to you. [6] But when you ask, you must believe and not doubt, because the one who doubts is like a wave of the sea, blown and tossed by the wind. [7] That person should not expect to receive anything from the Lord. [8] Such a person is double-minded and unstable in all they do. [9] Believers in humble circumstances ought to take pride in their high position. [10] But the rich should take pride in their humiliation—since they will pass away like a wild flower. [11] For the sun rises with scorching heat and withers the plant; its blossom falls and its beauty is destroyed. In the same way, the rich will fade away even while they go about their business. [12] Blessed is the one who perseveres under trial because, having stood the test, that person will receive the crown of life that the Lord has promised to those who love him. [13] When tempted[1], no one should say, "God is tempting me." For God cannot be tempted by evil, nor does he tempt anyone; [14] but each person is tempted when they are dragged away by their own evil desire and enticed. [15] Then, after desire has conceived, it gives birth to sin; and sin, when it is full-grown, gives birth to death. [16] Don't be deceived, my dear brothers and sisters. [17] Every good and perfect gift is from above, coming down from the Father of the heavenly lights, who does not change like shifting shadows.

---

[2] Trials and temptations are not sins in themselves, but our responses to them can be sin. *Trials* are difficult times that test our faith; we choose how to act and respond in the midst of them. They provide opportunities for either **sin** or faith, and they demonstrate whether our faith is real or not (1 Peter 1:7). *Temptations* occur when Satan entices us to do evil things. We are free to choose to give in to them or not.

▶ OBSERVE

*3. Discuss any words that are unfamiliar and then make a list of all the things this passage (vv. 2–12) says about trials and how to respond to them.

*4. Temptations are a specific kind of trial. List everything the passage says about temptations (vv. 13–15).

▶ INTERPRET

*5. James teaches us how to go through trials in a way that will help us see them as "pure joy." What does he tell us to do? What is the result of going through trials in this way?

*6. What do we learn about God from this text?

What is his role in our battle with trials and temptations?

▶ APPLY

*7. What trials have you experienced in the past and how did you deal with them?

What about now?

What kinds of trials might you experience after you graduate?

*8. Think about the times you were tempted in the past and how you responded. Do you still deal with these temptations? How do you need to face your temptations now? Share honestly with your group.

9. How do people from your home country usually deal with trials? And with temptations?

As a believer, how might you need to deal with them differently?

*10. How will you put what you learned into practice this week? With whom can you share and pray about trials or temptations you are facing?

RESPOND

Begin the practice of *thanksgiving*. Thanksgiving is not always easy, especially during trials and temptations, but it pleases God immensely when we praise him. In fact, Psalm 50:14, 23 and Hebrews 13:15 call thanksgiving and praise *sacrifices—* valuable offerings to God. Read Psalm 100. Find a blank sheet of paper or use a page in your devotional notebook and prayerfully begin a list of the things that you are thankful for. Continue this list all week and see how many things you can name. Fifty? A hundred? Each day, spend time in prayer thanking God for the new things you have added to the list. Watch to see how practicing thanksgiving changes your outlook on any trials or temptations you are facing.

Read the memory verse together.

 JAMES 1:2–4 (NIV) Consider it pure joy, my brothers and sisters, whenever you face trials of many kinds, because you know that the testing of your faith produces perseverance. Let perseverance finish its work so that you may be mature and complete, not lacking anything.

Write these verses in your heart language here:

Memorize them in your heart language and English this week.
Memorizing and quoting Scripture is a great way to battle temptations!

DIG DEEPER

○ Read more this week on what the Bible says about suffering and about thanksgiving as a sacrifice. Take time to study or meditate on the following passages:

- ▷ **Psalm 50:14, 23**
- ▷ **Romans 5:1–5**
- ▷ **Hebrews 4:15–16**

- ▷ **Hebrews 13:15**
- ▷ **1 Peter 4:12–19**
- ▷ **1 Peter 5:1–10**

○ Practice the discipline of fasting (see tips below). *Fasting* is the practice of not eating for a period of time in order to focus on God (Psalm 35:13; Acts 13:2–3). It allows believers to seek God through simply being with him, to know him more deeply through listening, to **confess** the things that keep us separated from him, and to be able to pray with more single-mindedness. Fasting also creates time to spend with God (for example, meal times are freed up) and teaches us dependence on him. Fasting is an excellent discipline to practice regularly. Start this week as you continue to think about the topics of suffering, temptation, and blessings.

▶ TIPS ON FASTING ◀

- ▷ If you have a health issue, consult your doctor before undertaking a fast. An alternative to fasting from food (for everyone, not just those with health issues) is to fast from media—such as TV, the Internet, and handheld technology—to spend the time focusing on God.

- ▷ Start small by skipping just one meal. Then, over time, work up to skipping all meals for a day, then for multiple days! Keep hydrated by drinking plenty of pure water.

- ▷ Instead of eating, spend time in prayer, Scripture reading, silence, and worship.

- ▷ While you're fasting, do not do things that simply distract you from being hungry; this is meant to be a time for you to draw near to the Lord.

CHAPTER
11

SPIRITUAL WARFARE

OPEN

- How did you put into practice what you learned from the Word last week?
- How did practice of time alone with God and thanksgiving go last week? How did you deal with trials and temptations differently?
- Take turns repeating the memory verse without looking at the guide.
- Pray briefly about what you shared and for your time in the Word.

 DIG IN

Ever since Satan, using the form of a serpent, deceived the first couple, he and the evil spirits under him have been fighting against human beings, particularly against God's people. But the good news is that Satan and his demons are created beings that are much less powerful than God. Jesus has already won the war over them in his death and **resurrection**, and our warfare is a "finishing up" operation.

In the Bible Satan is called the "prince of this world" (John 14:30 NIV). Although the world ultimately belongs to God, Satan does have great influence over it. All cultures reflect some aspect of the image of God, but they have all also been influenced by the enemy. And our old sinful nature, if we do not die to it daily, can give Satan an opportunity to influence us.

*So the **Christian** actually has three enemies: the "world" (human societies opposed to God), the "flesh" (our old sinful nature) and the devil or Satan. The term "spiritual warfare" refers to our ongoing battle against these three enemies.* God's intent is to heal all the relationships that were damaged when Adam and Eve sinned by disobeying him: relationships with God, self, others, and creation itself. Satan seeks to destroy or weaken those relationships.

*1. What do people from your country or cultural background believe about evil and evil spirits?

2. Take a few minutes to read through the texts silently. Mark words you do not know and questions you have. *Look for repeated words and ideas.

*Like the first woman and man, Jesus was tempted by Satan.
In this study we compare Jesus' response to Satan to that of the
first couple. In Genesis 2, God told Adam not to eat from one
particular tree in the middle of the garden and warned him that
he would die if he did so. In Genesis 3, Satan (using the form of
a serpent) questioned God's command. Rather than approaching
the man—who had actually heard God's command—he
approached the woman.*

GENESIS 3:1–6 (CEV)

¹ The snake was sneakier than any of the other wild animals that the Lord
God had made. One day it came to the woman and asked, "Did God tell
you not to eat fruit from any tree in the garden?" ² The woman answered,
"God said we could eat fruit from any tree in the garden, ³ except the one
in the middle. He told us not to eat fruit from that tree or even to touch
it. If we do, we will die." ⁴ "No, you won't!" the snake replied. ⁵ "God
understands what will happen on the day you eat fruit from that tree. You
will see what you have done, and you will know the difference between
right and wrong, just as God does."¹ ⁶ The woman stared at the fruit. It
looked beautiful and tasty. She wanted the wisdom that it would give her,
and she ate some of the fruit. Her husband was there with her, so she
gave some to him, and he ate it too.

---

¹ In verse 5, when the snake says, "just as God does," he is implying that the man
and woman will become like God, as some other translations make clear.

In Luke 3 we read that Jesus was baptized, heard the voice of his Father, and had the Holy Spirit come on him in the form of a dove. His Father's words were, "You are my own dear Son, and I am pleased with you" (3:22 CEV). After this powerful experience he went to the desert. In the Bible, it wasn't unusual for God's people to fast from food for a period of time in order to hear God more clearly and come close to him. Matthew tells us that the Spirit actually led Jesus into the desert so he could be tested and that Jesus fasted for forty days. Satan took advantage of Jesus' weakness (from fasting) and of the fact that he was alone. Adam and Eve failed their test; Jesus must be tested also.

LUKE 4:1–13 (CEV)

[1] When Jesus returned from the Jordan River, the power of the Holy Spirit was with him, and the Spirit led him into the desert. [2] For forty days Jesus was tested by the devil, and during that time he went without eating. When it was all over, he was hungry.

[3] The devil said to Jesus, "If you are God's Son, tell this stone to turn into bread."[2]

[4] Jesus answered, "The Scriptures say, 'No one can live only on food.'"

[5] Then the devil led Jesus up to a high place and quickly showed him all the nations on earth. [6] The devil said, "I will give all this power and glory to you. It has been given to me, and I can give it to anyone I want to. [7] Just worship me, and you can have it all."

[8] Jesus answered, "The Scriptures say: 'Worship the Lord your God and serve only him!'"

[9] Finally, the devil took Jesus to Jerusalem and had him stand on top of the temple. The devil said, "If you are God's Son, jump off.[1] [10–11] The Scriptures say: 'God will tell his angels to take care of you. They will catch you in their arms, and you will not hurt your feet on the stones.'"

---

[2] Satan already knows that Jesus is God's Son; the word *if* in verses 3 and 9 means "since."

¹² Jesus answered, "The Scriptures also say, 'Don't try to test the Lord your God!'"

¹³ After the devil had finished testing Jesus in every way possible, he left him for a while.³

▶ OBSERVE

*3. How are these two stories alike?
   How are they different?

4. What facts do you learn about Satan?
   About Jesus?

▶ INTERPRET

*5. What is Satan's goal in each situation?
   What strategies does he use?

*6. How did Eve and Adam lose the battle? Describe the steps.
   How did Jesus win?

_____

³ The three Scriptures Jesus quotes are all from Deuteronomy (8:3; 6:13; and 6:16), while Satan quotes Psalm 91:11–12.

▶ APPLY

This incident occurs before Jesus has begun his ministry and after he has heard a word affirming him as God's beloved Son (Luke 3:22). Some scholars believe that the devil is tempting him to use his powers as Son of God in the wrong way: to meet his physical needs and to obtain God's goal for him (to rule over the world) in a wrong way. In other words, these temptations highlighted wrong ways he could live his life and do ministry. The word if in verses 3 and 9 suggests that Satan may also be tempting Jesus to prove that he is the Son of God by doing something. But Jesus has just heard his Father's affirming word and knows his identity as a beloved child. He does not need to prove that identity to anyone

*7. Jesus will one day receive complete worship from the world, but the devil tempts him to obtain it by a shortcut that is wrong. Where do you see this kind of behavior in everyday life?

*8. When (present or future) might you be tempted to do this?

*9. In the Christian life we must do battle against our old sinful nature, the ungodly influences of the world around us, and the devil. Where are you most vulnerable right now?

10. How does what you learned from the text affirm and/or challenge aspects of the culture you're living in today?

The cultures you grew up in?

*11. How will you apply this to your life here and now?

How would this apply to your life back home?

RESPOND

This week's disciplines are **_confession_** and _accountability_. James 5:16 encourages us to confess our sins to one another and pray for one another. Our memory verse also tells us to give our worries to God. Schedule a special meeting time—in person or on the phone—with a Christian friend whom you trust. _Share with that friend a sin, problem, or worry that bothers you. Then pray together and agree to pray for each other. Plan to call each other a week later to see how things are going._ You might consider calling and praying on the phone weekly to continue confession and accountability. These practices can help you stay strong in the midst of spiritual warfare. If you already did this after last week's study on trials and temptations, talk to the friend you shared with, update each other, and pray again.

Your second assignment for this week is to _prayerfully prepare a "spiritual training plan"_ to share with your group next week. In chapter twelve we will see that the Christian life is like a long-distance race that requires training. Following a spiritual training plan is an effective way to become strong for spiritual warfare. Pray for the Holy Spirit's guidance as you fill in the worksheet below to make your training plan.

1. In what area(s) do you need and want to grow as a Christian? (God usually brings one thing to our attention at a time!)

2. What will your circumstances be like during the time you are following this plan?

    What will your schedule be?

    What special temptations or challenges might you meet?

Given these answers, choose a *few* daily and weekly practices from the lists below or others you are aware of. Some of the daily practices can be done during your time alone with God. Fill in realistic dates for the length of time you will follow this plan and the name of someone you will ask to hold you accountable.

YOUR NAME: DATES:

ACCOUNTABILITY PARTNER:

	YOUR CHOICES	NOTES
DAILY PRACTICES TIME ALONE WITH GOD *LECTIO DIVINA* INTERCESSION SCRIPTURE MEMORY PRACTICING THE PRESENCE		
WEEKLY PRACTICES ACCOUNTABILITY PARTNER STUDY/ACCOUNTABILITY GROUP CHURCH ATTENDANCE SABBATH KEEPING		
OTHER SHARING YOUR FAITH ACTS OF SERVICE FASTING		

If you are planning to return home soon, begin locating a church or group of Christians with whom you can fellowship now. It is important to attend church the first week you are back home if you possibly can. This sets a pattern for you and your family members. *Anticipate your new schedule* and ask God to show you bits of time—such as subway rides, driving, or even washing dishes—that you can use for prayer or meditating on Scripture that you have memorized.

Also, *consider continued accountability with current friends* through the computer or regular phone calls. This long-distance support can be helpful until you find good fellowship back home. *See "Tool G: Resources for Reentry" following this chapter for resources* to help you before and after returning home. Taking the time for spiritual practices may require great sacrifice and faith, but God will reward you as you seek first his **kingdom** and **righteousness**!

Read the memory verse together:

> **1 PETER 5:6–9 (CEV)** Be humble in the presence of God's mighty power, and he will honor you when the time comes. God cares for you, so turn all your worries over to him. Be on your guard and stay awake. Your enemy, the devil, is like a roaring lion, sneaking around to find someone to attack. But you must resist the devil and stay strong in your faith. You know that all over the world the Lord's followers are suffering just as you are.

Write these verses in your heart language here:

Memorize them in your heart language and English this week.

 **DIG DEEPER**

Bible study suggestions:

- What do **James 4:6–7** and **1 Peter 5:5–9** have in common? Why might humility be important in spiritual warfare?

- **John 8:31–44** gives more information about the devil and talks about how truth sets us free. **2 Corinthians 4:4** tells us what the enemy does to hinder non-believers from coming to Christ. Study these verses and then pray for the Holy Spirit to work in your mind and in the minds of non- believers you know, revealing truth and taking away blindness.

- **2 Corinthians 10:3–5** talks about the battle for our minds. Before becoming Christians, most of us had many lies in our minds. They don't all disappear immediately when we decide to follow Jesus. Some remain as strongholds that set themselves up against the knowledge of God. Satan can influence us through these lies. The Holy Spirit wants to reveal more and more truth to us as we learn Scripture and pray. Prayerfully ask God if there are lies you believe about God, self or life that need to be removed from your mind. Letting the Spirit bring to the surface and correct hidden ungodly beliefs in our minds is crucial in growing as a disciple.

- **Philippians 2:10, John 14:13,** and **Revelation 12:11** remind us of important weapons we have that can be used against Satan: the name and blood of Jesus (the blood stands for the finished work of Christ on the cross). If you ever sense an attack from an enemy spirit, call out to Jesus aloud and command the attacker to stop in Jesus' name.

- Read through the entire book of Ephesians. What truths about Christ's position (chapter 1) and our position (chapter 2) do you see? What commands (chapters 4, 5, and 6) can help us be victorious in warfare?

- The book *Sit, Walk, Stand* by the late Chinese church leader Watchman Nee (Christian Literature Crusade) looks at Ephesians in terms of the believer's life and warfare.

- *Spiritual Warfare in Mission* by Mary Anne and Jack Voelkel (InterVarsity Press) is a booklet that provides a succinct, biblical, and practical introduction to this topic.

- Our family and religious backgrounds, habitual sins and experiences of wounding sometimes make us vulnerable (open) to the attacks of the enemy. *Victory Over the Darkness: Realizing the Power of Your Identity in Christ* (Regal) and *The Bondage Breaker: Overcoming Negative Thoughts, Irrational Feelings, Habitual Sins* (Harvest House), both by Neil T. Anderson, provide practical steps to close these open doors.

- If you did not go to the Freedom in Christ Ministries website when you did chapter five, consider doing so now! Meditate on the identity statements found at: *www.ficm.org/handy-links/#!/who-i-am-in-christ*.

The books and identity statements mentioned above will help you become firmly grounded in your identity as a child of God and thus less vulnerable to enemy attacks.

RESOURCES FOR REENTRY

BOOKS & MATERIALS

- *Think Home: A Reentry Guide for Christian International Students* by Lisa Espineli Chinn. Available at the InterVarsity Store (*tiny.cc/t-home*).

- Overseas Campus *Returnee Handbook* (for mainland Chinese). Look under "Online Book" at *www.oc.org/web/*.

- *Putting the Bible to Work in Our Culture: Case Studies from Life Back Home* by John Eaves. Contains case studies that help you think through reentry issues in light of God's truth. Available at *www.intervarsity.org /ism/article/2044*.

- *Home Again* by Nate Mirza (NavPress). Written for Christian workers ministering to internationals but has valuable Bible study and resource suggestions.

- *Back Home: Daily Reflections on Reentry for Those Who Lived and Studied Abroad* by Lisa Espineli Chinn. Thirty devotions for the first month after reentry. Available at the InterVarsity Store (*tiny.cc/b-home*).

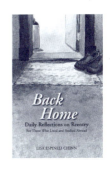

GROUPS & NETWORKING

- For connections with Christians back home, try the ACMI-Link (from the Association of Christians Ministering among Internationals): *www.acmi-net.net/acmi-link/*.

(continued on next page)

- Also visit the International Fellowship of Evangelical Students (IFES) website to find international student groups on college campuses in over 150 countries: *ifesworld.org*.

- The Japanese Christian Fellowship Network has conferences as well as fellowship and networking opportunities for Japanese Christian students in North America and back in Japan. See *jcfn.org*.

- If there is a church worshiping in your heart language near you, they could have many resources for you and may be able to connect you with Christians back home.

CHAPTER 12

VISION *for the* JOURNEY

OPEN

- How did you put into practice what you learned from the Word last week?

- How did practice of time alone with God and **confession** and accountability go last week?

- Share which disciplines you selected for your "spiritual training plan." Take turns repeating the memory verse without looking at the guide.

- Pray briefly about what you shared and for your time in the Word.

 DIG IN

The Old Testament paints a picture of the life of faith as a *journey*, and the New Testament adds the additional picture of a *race*. The best image for us may be that of a *marathon*, a long-distance race that might involve both running and walking. Finishing a marathon in good shape requires training, and the *I-DIG* has already introduced us to a number of training disciplines. In our final chapter we will look at passages from both the Old and the New Testament to get a clearer picture of the **Christian** life.

*1. What do people from your culture think about the existence of an unseen spiritual world?

*2. Take a few minutes to read through the texts silently. Mark words you do not know and questions you have. Look for repeated words and ideas.

*Hebrews is a sermon/letter written for Jewish Christians who were tempted to go back to the Jewish faith. At that time Christians were being imprisoned by the Roman government. After ten chapters demonstrating how living life with Jesus is far superior to the Jewish religion of repeated sacrifices, the writer introduces the idea of living by faith and gives examples of faith from the history of the **Jewish people**. Abraham was the father of the Jewish nation through Isaac and of other nations as well. Sarah was his wife.*

HEBREWS 11:3, 8–13; 12:1–3 (CEV)

[3] Because of our faith, we know that the world was made at God's command. We also know that what can be seen was made out of what cannot be seen....

[8] Abraham had faith and obeyed God. He was told to go to the land that God had said would be his, and he left for a country he had never seen. [9] Because Abraham had faith, he lived as a stranger in the promised land. He lived there in a tent, and so did Isaac and Jacob, who were later given the same promise. [10] Abraham did this, because he was waiting for the eternal city that God had planned and built. [11] Even when Sarah was too old to have children, she had faith that God would do what he had promised, and she had a son. [12] Her husband Abraham was almost dead, but he became the ancestor of many people. In fact, there are as many of them as there are stars in the sky or grains of sand along the beach.[1]...

[1] Such a large crowd of witnesses is all around us! So we must get rid of everything that slows us down, especially the sin that just won't let go. And we must be determined to run the race that is ahead of us. [2] We must keep our eyes on Jesus, who leads us and makes our faith complete. He endured the shame of being nailed to a cross, because he knew that later on he would be glad he did. Now he is seated at the right side of God's throne![2] [3] So keep your mind on Jesus, who put up with many insults from sinners. Then you won't get discouraged and give up.

---

[1] Abraham became the father of nations through both his sons Isaac and Ishmael (Genesis 21:1–13) and also of all people who trust in Jesus by faith (Galatians 3:29).
[2] The NIV translates verse 2 like this: "Let us fix our eyes on Jesus, the author and perfecter of our faith, who for the joy set before him endured the cross, scorning its shame, and sat down at the right hand of the throne of God."

▶ OBSERVE

*3. Discuss any words that are unfamiliar. Retell the text in your own words.

4. How would you summarize the main point of the text?

▶ INTERPRET

God had promised to Abraham that through him all the nations of the earth would be blessed (Genesis 12:3). Abraham and Sarah received one of God's promises, a son in their old age, but they did not live to see all nations of the earth blessed through Abraham. That promise was fulfilled in Jesus, a descendant of Abraham.

One of the background passages of Hebrews 11–12, Isaiah 35, paints a picture of the life of faith as filled with singing; this reminds us that there is also joy in the journey.

*5. How do the repeated words and ideas in the passage help you understand what faith really is?

6. What do we learn about faith from the examples of Abraham, Sarah, and Jesus?

*7. Based on these texts, how would you describe the Christian life?

▶ APPLY

In the time when Hebrews was written, following Jesus seemed shameful. Christians were misunderstood, insulted, and mistreated. Some had their possessions taken away, and some lost their lives because they followed Jesus. The same is true for Christians in parts of the world today.

*8. Look at the commands in chapter 12. Which is hardest for you?

What slows you down?

9. What would it mean for you to live by faith in various areas of your life?

10. How does what you learned from the text affirm and/or challenge aspects of the culture you're living in today?

The culture you grew up in?

*11. How will you apply this to your life here and now?

How would this apply to your life back home?

RESPOND

This week you will share with each other your "training for the race" plans that you prepared last week, pray for one another, and discuss next steps. Some may want to start a new *I-DIG* group and go through this guide with new friends. Others of you may want to continue this group for another 12 weeks using the facilitator's guide and suggestions for further study in Tool J. And some may be going home! Be sure to schedule a time to celebrate what you have done in the group (see "Dig Deeper" for suggestions).

Read the memory verse together:

 HEBREWS 12:1–2A (CEV) Such a large crowd of witnesses is all around us! So we must get rid of everything that slows us down, especially the sin that just won't let go. And we must be determined to run the race that is ahead of us. We must keep our eyes on Jesus, who leads us and makes our faith complete.

Write the memory verses in your heart language or another translation here:

Memorize them in your heart language and English this week.

DIG DEEPER

- Celebrate! Have a meal, dessert, or coffee together to celebrate finishing the *I-DIG*. Share words of encouragement about how you've seen each other grow, or give small treasures (cards, verses, photos) to each other. Don't forget to take a group picture!

- Read all of **Hebrews 11–12** to see the entire picture of the race of faith.

- **1 Corinthians 9:24–27** and **2 Timothy 4:6–8** provide pictures of how the early missionary Paul viewed the race during and at the end of his life. Study these verses to find additional wisdom and encouragement for the journey of faith.

- Read **1 Corinthians 10:1–13**, which suggests that we can learn lessons from the stories of the Jewish people in the desert. What things could become idols in your life? What might you be tempted to grumble about? How is 1 Corinthians 10:13 an encouragement? (It is a good verse to memorize!)

- *Daughters of Hope: Stories of Witness and Courage in the Face of Persecution* by Kay Marshall Strom and Michele Rickett (InterVarsity Press) contains inspiring stories of modern-day heroines of faith living in countries where following Jesus is often difficult.

- In some marathons, those who have finished early go back to walk beside their friends who may need some encouragement to finish the race. This is what Jesus does for us through the Holy Spirit. When you are feeling discouraged, spend some time in prayer and think about these words from **Hebrews 13:5b (NIV):**

    "NEVER WILL I LEAVE YOU; NEVER WILL I FORSAKE YOU."

GUIDELINES & NOTES FOR FACILITATORS

GETTING STARTED WITH THE *I-DIG* GUIDE

1. Make sure that everyone gets a copy of the guide in advance and reads "Discipleship and Digging: Introduction to the *I-DIG* Guide," "Getting the Most Out of Your *I-DIG* Guide," and "The I-DIG Group Meeting: A Preview" before your first meeting. Highlight key parts of these articles for yourself, so that you can mention them in the first group meeting.

2. During your first meeting, read aloud and discuss the commitments listed in "Getting the Most Out of Your *I-DIG* Guide." Agree together to these commitments for the next 12 weeks. If someone finds that they cannot attend regularly, ask them to attend one more meeting (at least the beginning of it) so the group can pray for them. Hopefully this will help them feel less awkward about not being able to continue and more likely to try again later.

3. If someone new joins the group within the first three weeks, have them read and agree to the commitments. After three weeks, close the group.

4. Your group can take turns facilitating or let one older Christian facilitate. You will grow more if you take turns. Each facilitator should read and follow the guidelines in this section.

5. Prepare each chapter in advance. Mark more important questions so that you can focus on them if time is running out (we have marked the ones we consider important with an asterisk [*]). The "APPLY" section is the most important, so be sure to leave plenty of time for that.

6. Find an older Christian who can advise you and answer questions. Ask this "coach" and additional people whom you recruit to pray regularly for your group and group members. Keep them informed!

7. Keep the meeting on schedule. You may need to shorten the passage or have fewer people share.

8. Invest in a pack of three-by five index cards. Take some to the meeting each week so people can write the memory verse on one side and record prayer requests for group members on the other side.

9. Don't be afraid of silence in the meeting. People need time to think about the questions.

10. Don't answer or comment on all the questions yourself. The goal is to help the group find answers together.

11. Here are some suggestions for common problems:

   ▶ Someone asks a question that's not related to the passage: Say, "Let's discuss this question after the meeting." If it's an important question, assign someone in the group to research it or talk to your coach.

   ▶ Someone gives a strange or wrong interpretation: Say, "Where is that found in the passage?"

   ▶ Someone shares from outside material: Say, "Let's focus on what our group is seeing."

12. Make sure the weekly facilitator has a copy of this guide and the notes for the appropriate chapter.

13. The I-DIG website tiny.cc/idig has a video and quick start guide to help your group get started easily. Coaches might want to watch the "Cultural Factors in Discipling" presentation.

◤ CHAPTER 1: FACILITATOR'S NOTES

OBJECTIVES OF THE STUDY:

- ▸ To help participants understand and start to experience the extravagant forgiveness, **grace**, and love of God the Father.

- ▸ To help students understand more deeply the difference between a personal relationship with God and religion based on performance.

- ▸ To help participants understand in particular that God's love is not dependent on our actions, no matter how much we have failed him or served him, and to understand the concept of grace.

- ▸ To provide an opportunity for students to turn from the "hired servant" or "older brother" mentality of working to please God.

NOTES ON THE QUESTIONS:

1. Pay attention to what the Holy Spirit is doing as you begin this I-DIG journey with your group (and every week). Relationships with fathers are often connected to much pain. Stop to pray if something important comes up, especially during the application time.

7. The younger son is like the tax collectors and sinners or outcasts. The older son is like the Pharisees and teachers of the law. In the story, the father

represents God. Jesus leaves the story unfinished because he is inviting the Pharisees to join God's party and celebrate that the sinners are coming home to God by spending time with Jesus.

9. This question provides a good opportunity to find out if everyone completely understands what it means to be a Christian. Try to keep stories short. If someone does not have a heart relationship with God yet, offer an opportunity at the appropriate time or meet with him or her later.

11. People from religious backgrounds where pleasing God or the gods involves performance often have difficulty deeply receiving relationship with God as a gift of grace. Listen to see if group members understand the difference.

◤ CHAPTER 2: FACILITATOR'S NOTES

OBJECTIVES OF THE STUDY:

- ▶ To help participants gain a deeper understanding of who Jesus is as a powerful member of the **Trinity**, not just a man with God-like characteristics.

- ▶ To remind participants that there will be people or ideas that tempt them away from believing Jesus fully during their lifetimes.

- ▶ To help students more deeply understand who Jesus is so that they will be "deeply rooted and firm in [their] faith" (Colossians 1:23 CEV). What confidence could be born if participants really believe in Jesus' authority and power!

NOTES ON THE QUESTIONS:

2–3. This passage is designed to highlight the complete authority of Jesus. The Colossians were beginning to trust false teachings that undermined Jesus' power; similar to cults today. Almost half of this passage is solely about Jesus (vv. 15–19). The rest is about us, specifically what Jesus did for us (vv. 20–22). There is also a stern instruction in verse 23 that is worth noting while sharing observations.

4. The power and authority of Jesus are key points to note in this passage.

6. To believe that Jesus has full authority and that he alone provides the path to eternal life would have brought freedom as well as power to the believers' lives and ministries.

◤ CHAPTER 3: FACILITATOR'S NOTES

OBJECTIVES OF THE STUDY:

- ▶ To understand the Holy Spirit's role. God brings action, revelation, and power to Christ-followers through the Holy Spirit, who lives inside each believer. It is vital for believers to understand that the Spirit's role is very significant!

- ▶ To begin to recognize, with the help of and dependence on the Holy Spirit, the places in our lives where we have sin and need to repent.

- To bring greater clarity to the mystery of the **Trinity**.
- To dispel any negative impressions of the Holy Spirit and to instead lead participants to long for more of him.

NOTES ON THE QUESTIONS:

5. The Spirit comes from the Father and the Son, testifies about Jesus, and brings glory to Jesus. He tells the believer what he hears from Jesus. He is in and with the believer. He helps, shows truth to, and teaches the believer. He reminds the believer of Jesus' words and speaks Jesus' messages. He convicts the world of sin.

8. He teaches truth and convicts.

9-10. The Holy Spirit is a person who loves us and with whom we have an ongoing relationship—a personal and dynamic relationship, not a mechanical one. This is in contrast to paying someone at a temple to receive guidance from the gods, for example.

◤ CHAPTER 4: FACILITATOR'S NOTES

OBJECTIVES OF THE STUDY:

- To know that we are the climax of God's creation and made in his image.
- To know that God loves us and wants to bless us.
- To understand the fall of human beings and the nature of sin.
- To see the difference between a life in which God is trusted and a life in which he is not trusted.

NOTES ON THE QUESTIONS:

5. Being made in the image of God implies that we have capacity for relationship (a kind that God could not have had with the animals, for example); we have the ability to love and be loved and to communicate at a deep level. Other implications: God is Creator; we can create. God is Ruler; we can rule (though not as well as he can). Note that verse 27 shows us that both male and female reflect the image of God (the NIV and other translations make this clearer).

7. All the harmonious relationships of chapters 1 and 2 in Genesis are broken: God with the people, Adam and Eve with each other (see v. 12), inside Adam's and Eve's own hearts (shame; see vv. 7 and 10), and people with the earth (vv. 17–18). Full of shame, guilt, and fear, these relationships no longer fully reflect the image of God.

   God is both just (giving a punishment) and merciful (providing the skins to clothe the people and promising a deliverer). (See v. 3:15.)

9. Answering this question could take a long time. Allow a few people to share and then suggest that people think about it later.

CHAPTER 5: FACILITATOR'S NOTES

OBJECTIVES OF THE STUDY:

- To help participants know that being a Christian means dying with Christ and receiving a new life that involves giving up old patterns and taking on new ones.

- To help participants start recognizing old patterns and be challenged and assisted in putting these to death.

- To aid participants in applying new patterns in their lives, beginning very practically with accountability from the group.

- To help participants know their new identity as children of God who obey out of love and gratefulness, not saved sinners who respond out of guilt or obligation.

NOTES ON THE QUESTIONS:

2. Death/life and taking off/putting on spiritual clothing are a few of the contrasts found in the text. You might suggest that people make a chart in the margin of their texts that shows the contrasts.

9. Our thoughts greatly influence our emotions and our behavior. Remembering who we belong to and who we are is a powerful tool for change.

CHAPTER 6: FACILITATOR'S NOTES

OBJECTIVES OF THE STUDY:

- To help participants realize that following Jesus means leaving everything in God's hands and that he is a good and trustworthy Father who loves us deeply.

- To help participants experience surrender and freedom through the application and "respond" challenge. Trusting in God is a major part of being a Christian. For someone who is new to following Christ, this could be a big challenge. Those people might need much prayer and accountability for each thing that is difficult to release.

NOTES ON THE QUESTIONS:

7. Believing that all they needed would be provided if they sought God's kingdom and righteousness first would have offered freedom from worry and a deepening of their faith. Seeking these things would have meant following God's leading in decision-making, knowing how to treat others, knowing what to do with their time and resources, and focusing on keeping their hearts and minds pure.

CHAPTER 7: FACILITATOR'S NOTES

OBJECTIVES OF THE STUDY:

- To help participants know that God cares about how we live our lives in relation to our families.

- To help participants begin talking about their families and romantic relationships in light of what they have learned.

- To aid participants in gaining new insight on what a good and godly marriage looks like.

- To challenge participants to begin letting God into their relationships and views on dating and put him first in these areas.

- To help participants see how their cultures do and don't agree with God's blueprint for families.

NOTES ON THE QUESTIONS:

5. Jesus' love for the church is the best example of sacrificial love there is. If husbands love like Jesus, it is easy for wives to respect them. But Paul also uses marriage to teach us about Jesus' relationship with the church.

6. The idea of a husband loving a wife as Christ loved the church, as well as the importance placed on the husband/wife relationship, would have been radical in that culture. It is still radical in some cultures today.

CHAPTER 8: FACILITATOR'S NOTES

OBJECTIVES OF THE STUDY:

- To help participants understand the power and importance of being involved in a Christ-centered community.

- To aid participants in recognizing the value of consistent involvement in church.

- To help participants understand what "church" is and isn't.

- To help participants develop a vision for what our Christian communities can be like: places where the Holy Spirit can bring wholeness, healing, and peace to people.

- To point participants to the fact that the I-DIG group is part of the church.

NOTES ON THE QUESTIONS:

7. This new church is quite radical. It emphasizes selfless community: sharing everything and being in total devotion to God. Imagine the difficult parts of this kind of oneness (for example, issues with impatience, ownership, and use of time).

9. The important components include baptism, regular learning from the Scriptures, fellowship, the Lord's Supper, caring for one another's needs, corporate worship, and sharing the gospel. Your I-DIG group has been practicing a number of these components, though not all.

10. Some students returning home may experience church culture shock. Churches are not the same around the world! Having future returnees imagine what their church experience will be like and remember the truly important components of a church can help prepare them. Remind them that worship and teaching styles are not the important components, and emphasize how essential it is that they connect to the church when they return home, no matter what its worship or teaching style is like!

◤ CHAPTER 9: FACILITATOR'S NOTES:

OBJECTIVES OF THE STUDY:
- To help participants gain a heart for the lost.
- To help participants see evangelism as essential to their faith.
- To empower participants to be salt and light to others here and back home.
- To give participants a sense of urgency for sharing their faith.

NOTES ON THE QUESTIONS:
5. Salt was used as a preservative as well as a seasoning in those days. Light enables us to see clearly and distinguish truth from falsehood. By their lives and words, Christians are to demonstrate the true nature of God and the true way human beings were intended to live on earth.

7. Jesus' compassion led him to heal people and preach the good news. It also led him to call believers to pray for workers for the harvest of people. The picture of people as harassed and helpless and the plentiful/few contrast give urgency to these verses.

◤ CHAPTER 10: FACILITATOR'S NOTES

OBJECTIVES OF THE STUDY:
- To help participants know that being a Christian does not prevent temptations and suffering and could actually cause them.
- To help participants make the connection that temptation is a part of suffering (though not a sin) and that our response to temptations is key to our receiving (or not receiving) blessings.
- To encourage participants be prepared for and unafraid of suffering and temptation, and to help them see the blessings they bring (perseverance, maturity, completion). (See James 1:2—"Consider it pure joy"—and Hebrews 12:2 for more help in understanding the blessings.)

- To help participants feel more prepared to go back to their home countries as believers.

- To help participants recognize our need for God's Word and help (wisdom) in battling temptations and facing trials. Without his help, we are possibly contributing to or causing other people's suffering and temptations.

NOTES ON THE QUESTIONS:

3–4. A trial is a test of our faith. God does not test people in the sense that he wants to see them fail. Rather, he "tries" or purifies us by testing to see where our faith and trust lie. Trials are designed to strengthen and refine us so that we grow strong and mature. Temptations are always trials, but not all trials are temptations.

5. *How*:

- Allow trials to produce perseverance in you.

- Ask God for wisdom in the midst of trials: asking for wisdom means also committing to obey whatever it is that God reveals. If there is no obedience, we are doubters.

- Ask in faith.

- Consider unseen spiritual truths, not just what you can see with your eyes (humble have a high position spiritually)

- Persevere–keep going–in the midst of trial

Result: maturity and completeness, crown of life from the Lord .Blessing comes through perseverance in the trials and temptations; our responsibility is to resist temptations, trusting that the blessings are better than anything the temptations could offer.

7. God is constant and steadfast and gives us hope. He also blesses us for our good responses to trials and temptations. In verse 17 he is called "the Father of heavenly lights" and the giver of every good gift. It is crucial to remember this, especially during trials and temptations when it could be easy to believe otherwise. This is a good verse to memorize!

◤ CHAPTER 11: FACILITATOR'S NOTES

OBJECTIVES OF THE STUDY:

- To help participants become aware of areas where they are vulnerable to attack from the enemy (from our sinful nature, from the influences around us (the world), and directly from Satan).

- To help participants see some of the strategies Satan uses to attack Christians.

- To show participants how Jesus defeated Satan and motivate them to follow Jesus' example.

- To encourage participants with the fact that Jesus was tested in every way we are.

  Facilitators, please be aware that different cultures will have extremely varied views on this subject. Make sure that conversations do not digress. If they do, get back to the passages chosen for the study by saying, "Let's see what we can learn from these passages."

NOTES ON THE QUESTIONS:

3. *Similarities*: Satan uses both lies and half-truths. He attacks the relationship with the Father. The test for both Adam and Eve and Jesus is whether or not they trust and obey God's word. The temptation in both passages is to become independent from God. Satan appeals to both physical and emotional desires.

   Differences: Satan disguises himself with the woman and does not do so with Jesus. Eve and Adam doubt God's word; Jesus remains in complete submission to his father's word because he trusts him.

4. *Satan*: Some of the facts you may not have noticed are that he uses half-truths as well as lies, knows Scripture well, and persists in his testing of humans.

   Jesus: He was tempted "in every way possible."

5. Satan's goal is to break relationship with the Father by getting the human to live independently of God and God's word. His strategy with Eve was to cause doubt about the goodness and trustworthiness of God by half-truths and lies. He also appealed to her physical senses and tempted her with the idea of being like God in a self-sufficient way.

6. Eve trusted the snake and herself rather than God. Adam, who was present and had actually heard God's command in person, did nothing to stop his wife. He trusted another human's judgment rather than God's.

   Jesus, secure in his identity as a child of his Father, didn't give in to the temptation to prove his identity by doing something. He knew God's Word so well that he could respond with appropriate Scriptures and speak the truth aloud to the enemy. Similarly, we need to be secure in our identity as adopted children of the Father and know Scripture well. We too may need to speak the truth aloud to the enemy when he tempts us.

8–9. Facilitators, please model openness by answering these questions honestly. Be accepting of whatever people share, and commit to help one another with areas of struggle. If the difficulty is beyond your ability, help your friend find an older Christian (perhaps a pastor, staff worker, or counselor) who can help.

◤ CHAPTER 12: FACILITATOR'S NOTES

OBJECTIVES OF THE STUDY:

- ◉ To help participants gain a realistic view of the Christian life as a long-distance journey that is filled with joy as well as challenges.
- ◉ To help participants understand the importance of faith in the Christian life.
- ◉ To encourage and inspire participants with the examples of Abraham, Sarah, and Jesus.

NOTES ON THE QUESTIONS:

5. Faith is seeing and living on the basis of the unseen God rather than on what can be seen. It is living based on God's promises. It may make us feel like foreigners in a world focused on the here and now and on what we can see.

6. Faith enables us to go through difficult times and bless many people. Like Abraham, Sarah, and Jesus, we can have many spiritual children by influencing others to become followers of Jesus.

7. The Christian life is a marathon, but we sing along the way—in other words, the journey involves both challenges and joy.

10. The advertising that we encounter everywhere keeps us focused on the seen world, especially things that please our senses or possessions that give us status.

WORD & CONCEPT LIST

apostles. In the Gospels the word refers to one of Jesus' twelve original disciples. In Acts and the Epistles the word has a larger meaning: a disciple specially sent by Jesus to share the gospel. An apostle had to be an eyewitness of Jesus after he rose from the dead. Paul's experience of Jesus on the road to Damascus qualified him (Acts 9:1–15; 1 Corinthians 15:3–8).

baptism. In the New Testament, baptisms were done by dipping someone under water as a sign of washing sin away. John the Baptist, the prophet who prepared people for Jesus, baptized people when they had a change of heart and mind and turned from sin to God. This change of heart and mind is called *repentance*.

Jesus commanded his disciples to baptize new disciples in the name of the Father, Son, and Holy Spirit (Matthew 28:18–20). Paul, when speaking of baptism, said that the act of going under the water and coming out of it is a sign of dying to sin and starting new life in God (Romans 6:3–11, Colossians 2:12).

For new believers, baptism is an outward sign of something God has done inside; *it does not bring salvation*. However, it is an important (usually public) testimony of who we are and an act of obedience to God.

Christian. A Christian is someone who follows Jesus Christ and believes that he is the Son of God, was sent to earth through a virgin birth, lived a sinless life, was killed, rose again from the dead, and lives now in heaven. Today the word *Christian* is often misused. A true Christian is not identified by a certain religious background or ethnicity or by how "good" they are. Instead, a true Christian can be identified as someone who has given his or her life over to God's control, obeys God, desires to become more like Jesus, and pursues Jesus' purposes in the world.

Note: Because people from certain cultural backgrounds may have an inaccurate idea of what the word *Christian* truly means, it may sometimes be helpful to describe yourself first as a "follower of Jesus" and then explain to friends or family what the term *Christian* really means.

circumcision. Usually circumcision is used as a medical term to describe cutting around the foreskin of a male's penis. Circumcision became part of the Jewish religion through an agreement between God and Abraham (Genesis 17). It was the physical sign God chose for any male who had agreed to participate in that covenant. From that day until now, all men and boys who choose to participate in the covenant of Abraham receive circumcision. Such persons are called "Jews." Should a non-Jewish male choose to become part of the Jewish religion, he would also be circumcised.

Because the Jews received the Law of Moses as part of their religion, *circumcision* came to apply to anyone who also lived by that Law. In the early years of Christianity, some followers of Jesus who were also Jewish thought that to be a Jesus-follower, you had to live by the Law of Moses as well as the teachings of Jesus, which meant you had to be circumcised. The apostle Paul disagreed. In Galatians 6:15 he wrote, *"Neither circumcision nor uncircumcision means anything; what counts is the new creation"* (NIV). This difference of opinion brought about a great debate among the early Christians leaders (see Acts 15). These leaders decided that Paul was right: it is not necessary to live by the Law of Moses and receive circumcision to be a follower of Jesus.

confession. To confess is to admit to God or another person something in your heart that is holding you back from a right relationship. As Richard Foster says in his book *Celebration of Discipline*, "At the heart of God is the desire to give and to forgive." If we do not confess, we set up a block to receiving God's gifts and forgiveness (see 1 John 1:9).

In the Old Testament, someone who wanted to ask for God's forgiveness needed to talk to a priest or offer an animal sacrifice (for example, see Leviticus 5:17–19). Now, since Jesus lived among people and left his Holy Spirit to be with us (see **Trinity**) anywhere and everywhere, we can confess freely to God without the help of a priest, though it can be helpful to do so with another person. Not only does sin need to be confessed to God to experience freedom and healing, but it also often needs to be expressed to another person who has been wronged or expressed *with* another person for accountability (see James 5:16). God's enemy, Satan, often uses brokenness in interpersonal relationships to make cracks in the church.

covenant. A covenant is an agreement between two sides in which one or both sides have an obligation to the other side. There are several covenants mentioned in the Bible. The most important covenant is God's covenant of grace with humans, in which God's obligation is to provide forgiveness of sins by grace, and our obligation is to receive that forgiveness by faith.

cult. A cult is a group that says they are Christian but does one or more of the following:

- *adds* something to the Bible, claiming another book is needed (for example, the Mormons add the *Book of Mormon*)
- *subtracts* something from what the Bible says about Jesus (for example, Jehovah's Witnesses say Jesus was not God)

- *multiplies* requirements for becoming a member of God's family and receiving eternal life (for example, Jehovah's Witnesses teach that obedience to their church commands are necessary to be a Christian)

- *divides* a person from friends and family, often by taking all their time and attention

These points are taken from Bill Perry's helpful pamphlet on cults: *They're Not Christian?? How to Identify Western Cults and Other Apparently Christian Groups* (Multi-Language Media, *www.multilanguage.com/feature.htm*). Read the entire pamphlet for more details.

disciple. A disciple is an apprentice, someone who follows an accomplished teacher to learn from and imitate them. The term is sometimes used for Jesus' twelve special followers. Discipleship is intentionally following Jesus as Teacher and Leader (Lord).

forgive. See "Tool F: Forgiveness" on p.79.

grace. Grace is the free, unearned, undeserved love of God given to human beings in practical ways, such as forgiveness for our sins and adoption into his family. Two verses that help us understand grace well are Ephesians 2:8–9 (NIV): "For it is by grace you have been saved, through faith—and this is not from yourselves, it is the gift of God—not by works, so that no one can boast."

inductive Bible study. This type of study allows you to discover the meaning of a Bible passage and apply it to your life by careful study. There are three kinds of questions:

- *Observation:* These questions help you discover what the passage says.

- *Interpretation:* These questions help you discover what the passage means.

  - In interpreting a passage, you need to consider the context of the verses, which includes the historical background and the material that comes before and after the passage in the chapter and book of the Bible. This helps you see what the passage meant to the original readers.

- *Application:* These questions help you discover what the passage means to you and how to apply it to your life.

For hints on how to do inductive Bible study, see *www.intervarsity.org/bible-studies/inductive-bible-study-hints*.

intercession. Intercession means praying purposefully for others with the hope that God will bring about good in their lives. It is very important in the life of the church because addressing problems and situations on the spiritual level will often bring about the healing, understanding, or answers that are needed in someone's life or a specific situation.

Jesus is our intercessor before the Father. The Holy Spirit is also an intercessor. When we pray, we can ask Jesus and the Holy Spirit to help us know how to pray and enter into their intercessions.

Jesus, deity and uniqueness.

How can we believe that Jesus is God? My friends say he's just a good teacher.[1]

The answer below is to strengthen you in your faith. Your friends will come to believe in Jesus as they get to know him through reading the Bible, putting his words into practice, and seeing how he changes you and other followers.

- ◗ Jesus says that he is God through his *words*:

  - ◉ John 10:30 (NIV): "I and the Father are one"; John 14:9 (NIV): "Anyone who has seen me has seen the Father."

  - ◉ John 8:58 (NIV): "'Very truly I tell you,' Jesus answered, 'before Abraham was born, I am!'" (I AM is the personal name for God that he gave to Moses in Exodus 3:14. After Jesus made this statement in John 8, the Jews picked up stones to throw at him because they recognized that he was claiming to be God.)

- ◗ Jesus also claims to be God through his *actions*:

  - ◉ Jesus forgave sin, something only God can do (see Matthew 9:2; Mark 2:5; Luke 7:48).

  - ◉ Jesus showed authority over nature (for example, he calmed a storm [Matthew 8:23–27; Mark 4:35–41; Luke 8:22–25] and walked on water [Matthew 14:24–33; Mark 6:45–51; John 6:16–21].

  - ◉ Jesus showed authority over diseases through his ability to heal (for example, he healed a nobleman's son [John 4:46–54], cleansed a leper [Mark 1:40–45; Luke 5:12–16], healed a paralytic [Matthew 9:2–8; Mark 2:3–12], healed a man with a shriveled hand [Matthew 12:9–13], and healed a man born blind [John 9:1–7]).

  - ◉ He had authority over death (for example, he raised people from the dead, like a widow's son [Luke 7:11–15], Jairus's daughter [Mark 5:22–43; Luke 8:41–56], and Lazarus [John 11:17–44]).

  - ◉ He showed authority over demons and the spiritual realm (see Matthew 8:28–34; Matthew 17:14–18; Mark 1:23–28; Mark 5:1–20; Mark 9:14–29; Luke 4:31–36; Luke 8:26–39; Luke 9:38–42).

- ◗ Jesus rose from the dead (see **resurrection** for Scriptures and details).

What makes Jesus and faith in him unique?[2]

Note: There are many *religions* that provide "paths to God" and experiences of various kinds. But only a living Jesus, raised from the dead, offers *relationship* with a living God both now and after we die.

- ◗ He was both fully God and fully human; no one else in history has claimed to be both God and man (John 1:14; Philippians 2:5–7).

- ◗ He was conceived by a virgin (Matthew 1:22–23).

---

[1] The answer to this question is taken from material compiled by J. L. West.
[2] These points are taken from "The Uniqueness of Jesus Christ" by Norman Geisler, available at *www.bethinking.org/jesus/the-uniqueness-of-jesus-christ*

- His birth (including his ancestry and place of birth), death, and resurrection were predicted by supernatural prophecies from the Old Testament (Psalm 2:7; Psalm 16:10; Isaiah 7:14; Isaiah 53; Micah 5:2).

- His life was filled with miracles that demonstrated authority (see previous question).

- He lived a life without sin of any kind (John 8:46; Hebrews 4:15).

- His life was a perfect example of love, compassion, and forgiveness (Luke 23:34, 43).

- He died and was raised from the dead; the founders of other great religions also died, but none of them has been raised from the dead (see **resurrection**).

- The salvation he offers is a free gift, not something humans must or can earn in some way (Ephesians 2:8–9).

Jewish people. The Jewish people began with Abraham, who is considered to be the "father" of the Jewish people. However, not all of the descendants of Abraham are Jews. The Bible mentions eight sons of Abraham, but only Isaac is also considered a Jew. Isaac in turn had two sons, and only one of them–Jacob, whose name was changed by God to Israel–is considered a Jew. All twelve sons of Jacob are regarded as Jews. One of Jacob's sons was named Judah, and it is from his name that we get the word *Jew*. The descendants of Jacob were not called Jewish people until 1,500 years after Abraham lived. The Jews were the people God prepared to receive Jesus.

In New Testament times most of the people in the areas where Jesus traveled were Jews. As a result, most of his ministry was to Jewish people, and his stories were about Jewish situations. There were also many Jews living in surrounding countries where the apostles, such as Paul and Peter, traveled.

kingdom of heaven or **kingdom of God**. These phrases refer to the rule or reign of God. There is both a present and a future aspect to the kingdom.

resurrection. *Resurrection* is the special word for Jesus' coming back to life after dying on the cross. It was:

- a resurrection of the body as a spiritual body, not capable of decay (1 Corinthians 15:42–44)

- not just a resuscitation (which is coming back to life but dying again)

- not a reincarnation (coming back to life in another form)

Disciples of Jesus will one day experience resurrection as well.

We believe in the resurrection because of:

- the empty tomb—the body of Jesus was never found (Matthew 27:62–28:7; John 20:1–9)

- the appearances of Jesus to his followers, who were not expecting him to rise again (1 Corinthians 15:3–9)

- the changed lives of those who saw Jesus (Acts 3:1–16; 1 Corinthians 15:8–10), many of whom later died for their belief in a resurrected Lord

- the witness of believers throughout history and our own experience of Jesus through the Holy Spirit

For more information, see the InterVarsity Press booklet *The Evidence for the Resurrection* by Norman Anderson.

righteousness. Righteousness means thinking and doing the right thing by God's standards. The ten commandments (Exodus 20) and examples from Jesus help us know what those standards are. True righteousness is not just in actions but also in the heart. Righteousness is granted through faith.

sin. Every human is born with a sinful nature (except Jesus, who is God). Simply described, sin is when we put ourselves in control. (Think of a "bad thing" or specific sin. If you trace its roots, you will see that it comes down to selfishness and a desire for power over someone or something.) Sin is what blocks us from God because he is perfect and holy, while sin is a spiritual disease. We first read about sin in the Bible in Genesis 3 when Adam and Eve eat the forbidden fruit in order to be like God. Since then, we have been kept at a distance from God, living apart from him.

Jesus was sent to the earth as part of God's plan to ultimately take care of our sin disease. Since sin keeps us from being with God, something needed to change in order for us to be able to be with him again. When Jesus, God's perfect Son, was killed on the cross, he died in order to pay the penalty for our sin disease. When he came back to life and went to heaven, Jesus proved that he is more powerful than anything—even death!

Trusting in Jesus, choosing to confess our sin to him and receiving his forgiveness, and asking God to be in control of our lives allows us to no longer live under the penalty of our sin, which is ultimate death and eternal separation from God.

Trinity. There is only one God and he is in three different persons—the Father, the Son, and the Holy Spirit (Matthew 28:19; Luke 3:21–22; 2 Corinthians 13:14). Each one is distinct, yet fully God. This does not mean Christians believe in three gods (see Deuteronomy 6:4 and Mark 12:29–30). This is a central belief in the Christian faith. Here are some helpful passages to see each person in the Trinity: Genesis 1:1–2; Isaiah 9:1–7; Luke 1:26–38; John 1:1–18; Acts 1:1–5; 2:1–47. *The Trinity, Practically Speaking* by Frank D. Macchia (InterVarsity Press) is helpful in understanding the Trinity better.

SUGGESTIONS & DISCUSSION GUIDE FOR ADDITIONAL I-DIG STUDIES:
BOOK OF EPHESIANS

TOOL

J

SESSION	EPHESIANS	SUGGESTED PRACTICE
1	1:1–14	Adoration
2	1:15–23	Intercession for friends.
3	2:1–10	Sabbath keeping.
4	2:11–22	Worship with a different racial or cultural group (one time).
5	3:1–13	Share your faith.
6	3:14–21	Secret acts of service or kindness.
7	4:1–16	Encourage a fellow Christian.
8	4:17–5:4	Make a forgiveness list and pray through it.
9	5:5–21	Share with an accountability partner.
10	5:21–33	Intercession for your spouse or for engaged or married couples.
11	6:1–9	Intercession for parents, children, or supervisors.
12	6:10–24	Pray through the armor listed in verses 13–17 and check in/ share with the same accountability partner from nine.

Along with your study of Ephesians, consider consulting or reading the following books:

- *Ephesians: Building a Community in Christ* by John Stott (InterVarsity Press), a Bible study that includes background information

- *Sit, Walk, Stand* by Watchman Nee (Christian Literature Crusade), an inspirational interpretation of Ephesians by the late Chinese church leader.

Continue to pray the Ephesians 1 and 3 prayers from the first *I-DIG* series for each other.

DISCUSSION GUIDE FOR ADDITIONAL I-DIG STUDIES

☀ OPEN (15 MINUTES) (10)

- ▶ How did you put into practice what you learned from the Word last week?
- ▶ How did your practice of the discipline go last week?
- ▶ Take turns repeating the memory verse without looking at the guide.
- ▶ Pray briefly about what you just shared and for your Bible discussion time.

⬋ DIG IN (55 MINUTES) (35)

1. Share background material about the Bible text from a study Bible (we recommend the *NIV Study Bible*) or commentary (try the *New Bible Commentary* from InterVarsity Press).

2. How do people from your culture view this topic? What are your thoughts about it?

3. Take a few minutes to read through the text. Mark words you do not know, items that impress to you or impress you, and questions you have.

▶ OBSERVE

4. Discuss any words that are unfamiliar and then take turns retelling the text using your own words.

5. What impresses you in the text?

▶ INTERPRET

6. What questions do you have? Answer the questions from the text and the context.

7. What would this text have meant to the original readers?

8. Try to summarize the passage in one sentence. What is the main point?

▶ APPLY

9. What do you learn about God the Father, Son, or Holy Spirit? About human beings in general? About yourself?

10. How does what you learned from the text affirm and/or challenge aspects of the culture you're living in today? The cultures you grew up in?

11. How will you apply this to your life here and now? How would this apply to your life back home? Whom will you ask to help you carry out this application?

RESPOND (20 MINUTES) (15)

- Decide on a spiritual practice appropriate to your text. Consider returning to one of the practices you tried out during the first 12 weeks of the *I-DIG* group.

- Choose a verse from the text to memorize and read it together.

- Close in prayer for each other.

NOTES

NOTES

AUTHORS

KRISTA MARTIN is team leader for the international InterVarsity chapter at the University of Oregon. She helped to plant the chapter there and learned a great deal about discipleship along the way. Growing up as a child of missionaries in Taiwan and traveling all over the world has given Krista a deep appreciation for all that international students experience during study abroad. Krista is married to Joel and they welcomed their son, Josiah, into the world in September 2012.

ERIC WU staffs an InterVarsity international fellowship that draws students from Pasadena City College and East LA College in the San Gabriel Valley of California. Eric, who has been on staff for over ten years, has discipled many students who have just become Christians. He recently had the joy of seeing one of his students become the InterVarsity International Student Ministry (ISM) staff worker at a nearby university.

Eric and Krista worked on the *I-DIG* as part of their participation in the Daniel Project, an InterVarsity leadership development program.

KATIE RAWSON is senior resource developer with the InterVarsity International Student Ministry (ISM) Department. Experience as an international student in France led her to ISM with InterVarsity, and she has served at both North Carolina State University and UCLA. During more than thirty years of ministry Katie has seen some international students grow to maturity and fruitfulness and others stall in their Christian lives, so she has a passion for equipping people to finish the journey with Jesus well. Katie, who has doctorates in French literature and cross-cultural communication, lives in Raleigh, North Carolina.